Biggest
Fullest
Brightest

Shifting the Consciousness of Humanity

Bolden Fields Publishing/Bolden Fields, LLC
Bowie, MD 20715
www.boldenfieldspublishing.com

Library of Congress Control Number: 2022920519
ISBN 978-0-9907201-3-3 (paperback)
ISBN 978-0-9907201-4-0 (eBook)

Editor's note:
This publication is not intended as a substitute for advice of healthcare professionals.

Final interior design and typesetting by Bolden Fields Publishing, LLC

"Biggest Fullest Brightest took me on a journey of self growth. It guided me to ask myself difficult questions that changed my perspective of the world around me and the world inside my mind. Matthew's ability to share his core being while guiding the reader through self exploration exercises connects on a level that is foundational. Building on that foundation is up to the individual reader. Growth can be exponential with this book as a guide. I keep this book handy and continue to review and adjust the exercises as my personal goals advance."
—Ethan Reynolds

"...To say reading Matthew's book was an eye opener is an understatement…Matthew's book made me aware that everyone needs to take a personal assessment of where they are and how far they still need to go. …My dear friend has shared his story and, even though I thought I was pretty much finished with my evolution, made me aware of my own journey awaiting my first step."
—LaJuana Berdanier

"Matthew's book found me at exactly the right time and place. I felt so seen as I read the purposeful words in this book, and nearly every chapter brought me an unexpected revelation. Biggest, Fullest, Brightest is for everyone. It was an honor to be a part of this invaluable and powerful book's birth into the world."
—Kelsey Sutton

"What starts as a personal exploration story, quickly grows into a designed roadmap of how to show up in the world, regardless of your past. Peppered in the story are reflective journaling prompts, [which] allowed me to delve into how much of my thinking is generated by me. Matthew's journey in life and the work he has done to heal is a snapshot of what one person can do to help collectively shift mankind into a kinder, more loving world."
—Robin Reames

Biggest Fullest Brightest

Shifting the Consciousness of Humanity

Matthew Reynolds and Brittnee Zwirn

DEDICATION

I dedicate this book in loving memory of Glenda Lou Reynolds and Emanuel Reynolds. May you be speaking with the ancestors, guiding me as I continue to shift the consciousness of humanity towards a more human-led world.

table
of contents

I met Matthew at my first teaching job. I was struggling to fit my ideals of education into an educational system that continued to push, pull, and stifle students. I felt like I was a cog in a system that I did not believe in or want to be a part of. I felt excited to be part of a school where students were different and seemed to want to be there. However, I noticed that a lot of my students were frustrated, disengaged, and focused solely on the grade. It was discouraging and disappointing. Then I started to notice that Matthew's students were different. They were excited to be at school, took charge of their education, and ignored the times the system tried to mold them into people they did not want to be. They knew what it meant to be their biggest, fullest, and brightest and they radiated that for all to see.

I knew this was what I wanted for my students and students everywhere. I spent more time talking with Matthew and watching him teach. We started dreaming about what we wanted the education system to look like and then Matthew would always challenge me by saying, "Why can't you do that in your own classroom?" or "So, do it." I knew he was right, but often I felt this need to stick with the status quo. That pull of what is comfortable, what has always been done was too easy. It is so much harder to fight against it.

Slowly, I did and am still trying to create the dream of a more humane educational system in my own classroom.

These movements, conversations, and challenges sparked our conversations to shift to dreaming about one day starting our own school. So when he came to me and said, "Will you help me with this book?" I enthusiastically said "YES!" Internally, I said, "Phew … this will be easier than starting our own school" (although, now this is debatable).

What started out as me helping Matthew get words onto paper turned into a collaborative sketching of what this book could be and what the impact of these words would be on society and the future generations. The memories and philosophies are all Matthew's, but there were so many times I found I was contributing or building on those ideas from my own perspective. I did this by remembering conversations we had in the past or by talking about our ideals and typing my thoughts onto each page. The more we wrote the more I started to see how I could take these ideas and stop dreaming–and instead start living them.

With the help of my own Equity Lens, first crafted in my second-year teaching during a lunch conversation with Matthew and then refined in Matthew's workshop, I was empowered to make my dreams a reality. Throughout the work on this book, we often found that the chapter we were working on directly aligned with what was going on in the world around us, within ourselves, or with our friends and family. This only confirmed that what we were creating together was going to be important for the world.

This book is important because not only does it ask you to confront white-bodied supremacy culture, but it also asks YOU to do the WORK. So often white people (myself included) read, attend workshops, watch talks about anti-racism/equity and think, "Well my job is done! I have become an ally!" Our job is not complete and "we" haven't become allies. "We" did not do the work to untangle the threads of white supremacy that are so intertwined with everything that we do. There is a need to start moving towards becoming an accomplice; one who actively works with others to help dismantle a system that is oppressive to all.

This book helps you to start to do that. This book gives you tools to really reflect about your role in the perpetuation of white-bodied supremacy culture and to urge you to do something about it. It is Work, but this is meaningful, scary, exhilarating, and important. This Work will help you to take ownership of your thoughts, actions, and education. This Work will encourage you and remind you that YOU MATTER. This Work will also challenge you and beg you to grow and change in ways you never thought possible. This Work will allow you to be your biggest, fullest, and brightest.

Dear Human,

I want to invite you on a journey of sorts. But before we do that, there are a few things I must explain to you. I'm not here to tell you how to live your life, what is and isn't important in your lived experiences, or how you are to deal with obstacles that have seemingly taken the breath out of you when they come up in your world. This is an invitation. An invitation to begin exploring who your authentic self truly is.

One of the ways I personally began this journey is through the perspective of the spiral. The spiral is life because it never remains the same. There are different places within it that teach you about yourself. From life's lessons, the spiral allows you to return to its center — feeling grounded.

There have been moments in my life when I felt this great sense of groundedness. Like being at one with myself, if you will. These moments have happened when I wasn't trying to fit into a situation like a party, a classroom, family time, and/or a job. There was an ease about being in this skin of mine, having these thoughts, feeling the love I have toward others. All seemed so real and uncontrived. The center of the spiral.

But it isn't easy to stay in that center. Staying in the center of the spiral is a balancing act and can be even harder if one isn't self-aware. As a minute or hour might have it, "life" happens and knocks you a little off course. Someone yells a racial/homophobic/ableist/sexist slur at you, not recognizing your humanity.

–SHIFT–

Moving off of that center and possibly even beginning to rotate slowly, you move out onto the arms of life, spiraling out from the center.

It has begun.

The person you have a crush on not only doesn't like you back, but also threatens violence, while screaming at the top of their lungs, "I AM NOT GAY!"

–SHIFT–

Your job tells you that you are an incredible employee, but that they just don't have enough hours for you, and since you were the last one hired, you are the first one fired.

–SHIFT–

Your parents are constantly arguing about anything and everything. You are constantly walking on eggshells around them because you don't want another fight to occur. You internalize this, and as you get older you wonder why it's hard to find someone to date.

–SHIFT–

You were bullied as a child because you were overweight. You developed an eating disorder. You continually think that you must lose weight to fit into the beauty standards the world tells you to uphold.

–SHIFT–

Next thing you know, several of these SHIFTS are happening simultaneously. You are spinning further and further away from the center. Your clothes are disheveled, but you get dressed and put on the facade that everything is alright. Meanwhile, you are spinning faster and faster. Fighting hard now to fit in, make it work, believe what they told you. "If you work hard, you can accomplish anything you want." You are working hard, so damn hard. You wake up in the middle of the night and you don't know who the fuck you are anymore.

This last SHIFT takes your feet out from underneath you. You are holding onto the arm of the spiral with just your fingertips. Your entire body is flapping in the wind, as if you were laundry out to dry. If you squint really hard you can see the spiral your life has been. A spiral out and away from center, and center seems really far away right now.

Some of us never find our way back to the center.

Others of us numb ourselves into believing we are at the center again. We have such deeply rooted masks that cover pain, trauma, acceptance of self, and basic everyday feelings. We forget there even was a center to get back to.

And even still others of us find tools. Tools that give us insight into the grounded center of the spiral. This book describes some of those tools. It is completely up to you to choose whether or not to pick them up, adjust them to your grip, and use them. I am inviting you to do exactly that.

On this journey you will be asked to write out your own story, which may be similar to the one I share or to respond to a prompt, asking for your truth. None of this is going to be shared unless you choose to, but know that I am not asking you to. I am inviting you to participate. There are also interactive moments, breathing exercises, reminders to hydrate, moments to listen to a song, get up and stretch, walk, run, dance, wiggle, breathe. You may feel inspired to come up with some of your own cell-shaking moments. Please, do them. Somatic Healing is approaching our healing of trauma through our bodies. You know you are moving forward in your personal healing when you literally start moving. Restless limbs, fidgeting fingers and toes, areas of sudden warmth, itchiness, and so forth. I ask that you journal about it, these moments, and take the notes with you to a somatic healer.

Within these pages there is the power of language. Some words I use have definitions shaped by my lived experiences and subcultures, and they are pieced together for a deeper connection to those with whom I am speaking. If you do not understand a word, chances are it will be defined more deeply in another chapter.

All of these tools, in their own way, will help keep you from spending too much time flapping on the outer edges of your spiral. Don't get me wrong, as you will learn in the coming pages, the outer edge has a lot to offer a person, if you let it. Spending too much time stressed out only shortens your life while raising your cortisol levels. Being grounded is another way of helping yourself to be balanced in mind, body, and spirit.

Remember, you are not alone. You are loved, and you are love.

ENJOY the journey.

amerikkkan dad

The extension cord has a distinct sound
Whizzzzzzzz shlack Whizzzzzzzz shlack Whizzzzzzzz shlack
I am transferring myself to another place
A place where the sting isn't so great
In my nine-year-old head, I am repeating over and over again
I didn't mean to make you so mad
I didn't know it was a bad thing to eat at the neighbor's
I didn't do it to make you look like a bad father

Shame. Absorbed into my psyche oh so quickly oh so easily

I hear you on the phone
You ask the same question twice, "What did he call you?"
Nowhere to run
"What did he call you?"
Nowhere to hide
This time it is the yardstick, not as sting-y, leaves a different welt
He called me that "little nigger boy"
Did he tell you that part, Dad?!?
Did he?!?!

Shame. Absorbed into my psyche oh so quickly oh so easily

What demons from your upbringing were you exorcizing
How many were there, for you to beat me so
What, you won't talk about those times in your life
You aren't going to give me anything to go off of to forgive you

In these moments, you really were a fucking, shitty father
Your parenting was so fucked up
And …
I love you

Shame. Absorbed into my psyche oh so quickly oh, so easily
Let me give myself some grace

I am the fourth child of six, son of Glenda Lou Sorrells and Emanuel Reynolds Jr. From my mother, I am Irish, German, and Swedish. My father was second generation out of slavery. Some would call him African American. He would call himself a Black man. My parents met almost a decade before the *Loving v. Virginia* Supreme Court decision[1]. My mother was kicked out of her house and disowned by her family for dating a Black man; my father. They began the trek North, where things were supposed to be better for an interracial couple such as themselves. This turned out to not be true for their six kids and, for all intents and purposes, it wasn't for them either.

I started fighting when I was three years old. My mother taught us four older kids that if anyone called us the n-word, we were to respond with a punch in the mouth. I saw my mother respond this way on several occasions, for something less than the n-word. When I got into that fight, it started a conversation with my parents about moving out of the cities, Minneapolis, and into the country. My father wanted to have his own TV repair shop, and my mother wanted to have her own garden, just like when she grew up. We moved to Isanti, Minnesota.

At the time, the town had a population of around 1,500, and we were the only interracial "family of color" until I reached the eighth grade. So it began, more fighting. From the age of three to fourteen, I fought at least three times a week and sometimes all five days at school, with the occasional fight on the weekends when we were still living in town. "Friends" would be playing with me and my older brother. They'd lose a game and out would pop the n-word, and out came my fists. It was tiring. This continued through the eighth grade and became worse when I realized I could not keep my attraction to other males a secret anymore. I came out at the age of twelve, while fishing along the Rum River with my friend.

"I think I have a crush on your older brother?"

"I think that is just a phase. You'll get over it," he responded.

Funny that a twelve-year-old would have that response. This started my journey of dealing with my own internalized homophobia.

My father didn't handle his internalized racial oppressions well at all. He was what I would call your typical '50s father. He put a roof over our heads, clothes on our backs, and food on the table. That was what he did, and that's all he did. He never asked how I was doing or came to any of my school events or conferences until my senior year. He was also physically and mentally abusive toward me. I was called lazy, a liar, a trouble maker, disrespectful, and, in my judgment, too much like my mother. I would be struck with his hand, an extension cord, a yardstick, or asked to cut a switch from the bush in the backyard. All of this while he reeked of alcohol. Yeah, he didn't have any resources to call upon that would enable him to talk about being a Black man, in love with a white woman, living in rural Amerikkka, in the North. Oof. It took me years to understand this, and he died before I had the tools and the courage to talk with him about any of it. Plus, I was going through my own shit. By the time I graduated from high school, I had tried to take my own life three times. The pressures of society, name calling, beatings at home, were so much that taking my own life was a constant thought in the back of my mind. There was literally no place for me to release any of this pressure, to feel safe, and/or feel like I belonged. The voices telling me to be something I wasn't were all too overwhelming, confusing, and had me consistently on the outer edges of the spiral. Every time I tried to take my own life, I wasn't successful, and even that added to the stress. Today, I can say that I am glad I am still here.

I was so excited to get to college, so I could be around more Black and Queer folks. Sadly, that was all shattered rather quickly. You see, I was too "white" for the Black people that I met.

"You talk white!"

"You dress white!"

"You sure you don't want to be white?"

The gay community wasn't any better. I didn't know anything about the queer subculture, and that meant I was an outsider. I had nowhere to belong, and after all the shit I went through growing up, I couldn't handle this, too. This is when I first came to the decision that I would create my own place of belonging. A place where I can bring ALL aspects of me to the table, room, trip, and life!

What could I build with this life of mine if all of me was lovingly supported by the world around me? What could I achieve? How would I thrive? Little did I know at the time that I was formulating my philosophy of education, and how that would govern my classrooms, my writing, and my purpose in life.

Becoming a licensed educator was a moment in life that illuminated my soul. It was as if I could look over my shoulder and peer into my past, seeing connections of lived experiences that pointed me to right where I was as an educator. No longer did I see my past as a thing that held me back. Now, I could see how the past was made up of moments of learning, allowing me to be here (in the middle of my spiral) grounded in who I am. No going back to old patterns that did not serve me.

Sometimes in life we are hit with soul-illuminating experiences: deep conversation, new job, falling in love, near death. These experiences shift us to the core and afterwards, there's no going back to old ways of thought.

Which lived experience has opened your eyes to a new way of being? Please share one time this occurred for you.

It is important to know your personal history.
Don't recoil, or regret.
Open up.
Face it.
Embrace it.
It is all you,
all of it,
so learn from it.
From that understanding comes wisdom.

This wisdom helps us to reach the furthest most shores in our personal journeys.

I have done a lot, and I mean a LOT, of personal Work around my physical abuse from my father. I have also had to work through growing up in a predominantly white town/environment, being gay, and being multi-ethnic. The trauma I haven't dealt with is how all of this has affected my outlook on Black men, and more so on how I view myself as a Black man. I cared deeply for my father when I was young. I longed for his loving attention, which included just showing an interest in me as his son. When I was out of the house, and well on my way to living *my* journey, he began to show some interest. You see, he was dying, and his faith told him he must make amends. I didn't want to hear it. The damage had been done, and I had moved on with my life and my healing. At that time, my life didn't involve him.

Now?

I would love to sit and talk with him about his life. What was it like growing up in Montgomery, Alabama? What was your family like? Who were your friends? Were there stories told of being enslaved? Did you know where the land was that your family worked? Does our last name, Reynolds, come from a slave owner? How did the answers to these questions form you into the man you were? How did you get the notion to leave there? Did you really love my mother, or was she a means to escape the South? How do I be a Black man? How do I be a gay, Black man?

All of this has made me want to reach for the miracle of belonging. You see, I don't feel like I truly belong anywhere. Including, at times, to myself. I let this wound, these lost moments, take over my sensibilities and *WOOSH*, I am whisked away to *UNWORTHYLANDIA!!* A place that doesn't see any worth in any part of me. And my dreams of belonging pull me back, sometimes kicking and screaming, to this place I am building for others . . . Yes, and for myself. I am "dreaming belonging" into being.

True Belonging

True belonging is the spiritual practice of believing in and belonging to yourself so deeply that you can share your most authentic self with the world and find sacredness in both being a part of something and standing alone in the wilderness. True belonging doesn't require you to change who you are; it requires you to be who you are.

– Brené Brown[2]

I learned from Dr. Brené Brown that the strongest desire of the human mind is to have a sense of belonging. Once I read that, I knew that this feeling, this desire I've had all my life, is a deeply rooted part of being human. The quote above fills my imagination with all the possibilities for humanity. What if we all felt like we could bring our authentic selves ANYWHERE we went! The clarity it would bring to communication, expressing our wants and desires, setting boundaries, and putting out unconditional love into the world. THAT is magic! THAT is being human.

What was your initial reaction when you first read the quote on true belonging? What stands in your way of believing in and belonging to yourself?

Invitation: Find an accountability buddy. Share Brené Brown's quote with them. Talk about your answers to the above questions and make a plan to begin walking the journey of true belonging. Find your magic, and LIVE IT! Let us start to see what kind of a world we can build with all of us feeling, living, breathing our true belonging.

True belonging doesn't just show up one day. It takes self-determination, introspection, and a deeper connection to your authentic self. One of the biggest blocks to true belonging, for me and others, is the construct of racism.

During the election of 2020, when someone said "racism" was what went to the polls, it caught in my chest and I couldn't breathe. The realization washed over me. All of my life has been led by racism. The depth of internalized racial oppressions, genetically modified hundreds of years ago, surges thunderously through my blood, my cells, wreaking havoc on my soul, cellularly feeling the middle passage of slavery, and slams into the shores of the great void, the shores where my ancestors were bought and sold. How do I forgive the United States of Amerikkka? Enslaving my ancestors, creating *white*, creating racism, creating a story that bestows privileges to white persons for generations and persists today creating themselves as the "dominant culture." The impact on me tumbles through my internalized racial oppressions. I will never know what a complete me is capable of. But how can I miss what I never had?

Invitation: Let's take a breath here. Sitting up tall, or standing tall, allow your spine to feel as if it extends down into the core of the earth and out into the infinity of space. All of your skin, organs, bones are all free from gravity and being suspended by this thread reaching in either direction, out into the infinity of space, and deep into the earth's core. If the shape of your body doesn't allow for your spine to feel like it is extending out in both directions, please utilize your mind's eye to envision this happening.

Slowly let your vision come into a soft focus, allowing your sight to look inward. Your lungs are three-dimensional. I want you to take your hands and trace the bottom of your rib cage. Again, this might be achieved with the guidance of your mind's eye. Your rib cage protects your lungs. Feel how far down on your body it goes, and how it goes all the way around to connect with your spine. Allow your hands now to drift away to your sides, or come to rest on your thighs. Filling up your lungs from the bottom, inhale deeply, while envisioning the width and depth of your lungs. Allow them to fill up as if you were pouring water into a bucket, filling from the bottom up, filling up in all directions.

Once filled, hold for a slow count of four. With a hisssssss, exhale slowly. Keep pushing until you have gotten all the air out, and then hold for a slow count of four. Inhale and repeat the process three to five times.

Allow yourself to breathe without any counts or other enhancements. Let your focus come back into the room. Feel the thread reaching into the earth, and out through the Universe, arrive back home as part of you. Sit quietly for five to ten minutes and observe your body. Please take some time and explain how that was for you. Notice tension in the body, images and/or colors in your mind's eye, memories wanting attention, tingles, itches, goosebumps, and so forth.

You can always return to this breathing exercise whenever you feel this tool may be helpful in your daily life as well.

The first couple of times I did this breathing exercise, I was fixated on how large my lungs actually were! Now, while I do it, I have these moments where I am somewhere in the history of my bloodline; from full imagery, to rushes of feelings and emotions. Every time has involved racism. I didn't know what was going on with me until I learned about epigenetics. My understanding of epigenetics is when there are changes to the physical structure of DNA, which prevents certain genes from being expressed, thus altering the way in which you might respond to trauma(s). When I learned of this, I decided for myself that I wouldn't refer to this as something negatively passed along to me. I decided to call them "gifts."

RELEASE … Letting go of the "gifts" passed along to me through epigenetics.

I'll try to give more details as to why I say the words I say, in the manner in which I say them, as they occur. The language I am using comes from my lived experiences and may seem foreign to you. I talk from my heart and how I would speak if I were in a conversation with you. Also, I talk with the voice in my ear saying, "Wow! You speak really well." That statement has come from white-bodied folx who think that a Black man shouldn't sound so learned. Another voice in my ear is saying, "Damn, you sure talk white!" This has been some Black folx way of saying that I've been "whitewashed," that I wish I were white.

After all this time, I talk like Matthew. Those voices, created by my lived experiences, feed my negative self-talk, which in turn feeds what I call my Shadow. Over the years, the best defense I've come up with to combat these voices in my ear is to ask myself the question, *How much of your thinking is your thinking?* I still ask myself that question, actually, and more frequently as I recognize my internalized racial oppressions. These are concepts of self, frequently negative, that have been fed to me through my indoctrination into the status quo. Knowing this about myself, I now ask that question to those around me, my students, colleagues, acquaintances, clients, everyone who I feel is upholding ideas of white supremacy culture, knowingly or unknowingly, myself included.

Breaking down the constructs of Amerikkka starts with personal Work. Educate your mind, feed your soul. When I make this statement, it isn't because I want everyone to get on the bandwagon and think just like me. My statement is (or my statements are) to encourage everyone to critically THINK about what facts, truths, and lived experiences are being presented, and how they manifest within your mind, body, and spirit. Then ask yourself, *How much of your thinking is your thinking?* Our humanity is buried deep beneath a lot of white supremacy culture. That's culture that has been constructed through ALL inventions of colonialism, religion, capitalism, and many other constructs that have pulled humans away from humanity. Now, I am grateful for your journaling, the education here, and the ability to think critically about ourselves. I am interested, though, in what we can build to shine a brighter light on helping each other lead with our humanity.

Please answer the question: *How much of your thinking is your thinking?*

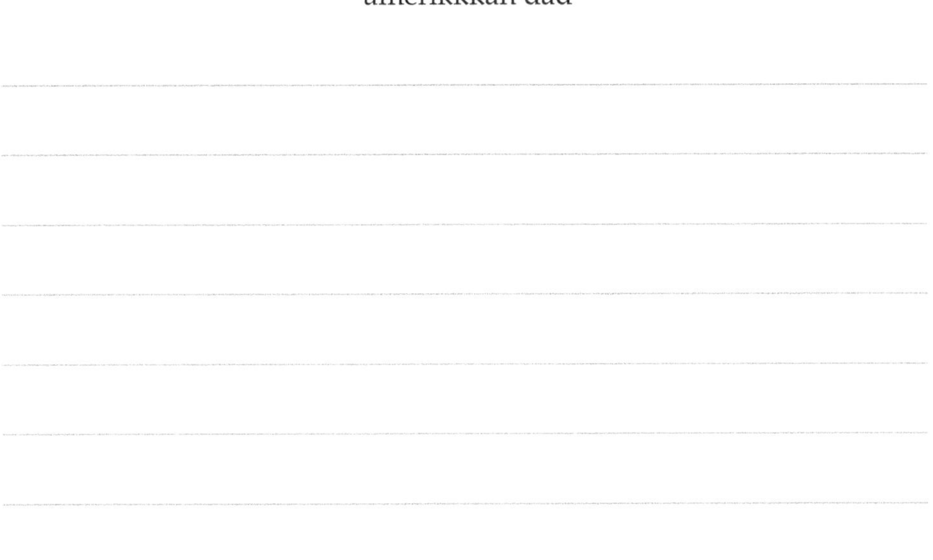

Thank you for speaking your truth — *Speak your truth*. With that comes a direct need for self-reflection, a desire to learn, and many hats: mentor, teacher, learner, knower, parent, guide, bank, and so forth. (I put "bank" as a hat I've worn because I 've often given students who could not afford things money so that it wasn't a barrier to their experiences.) It's important for us as humans to model for other humans what it is that we expect from them, and if we cannot model that behavior for them, well, then maybe we need to rethink what our actions might have been in certain situations. Speaking our truth helps us create a space where shame and fear do not rule the space, but rather those things are allowed to be looked at and unpacked with everyone involved. Speaking our truth helps us to find our own humanness.

Amerikkka: this is how I distinguish us from North Americans, Central Americans, and South Americans, the Americas. I spell it this way because, out of the constructs of white, whiteness, race, and racism, was born the Ku Klux Klan. Those who colonized North America created all of these constructs, which led the way to a domestic terrorist group trying to uphold those lies, thus **Amerikkka.**

When white-bodied Amerikkka wanted to see, wanted to

wake up, wanted to fight against all of this, everything that I have been speaking to up to this point, internalized racial oppressions, they had no idea what they were in for. Let us see it all, so we know what not to build again. Let us see it all, so we can get the depths of this poison up and out of us. Let us see it all, so our healing is complete. Then, and only then, will we begin to leave something better for seven generations from now. This is Work. Are you really ready for it? Or will we wallow in our comfort? The way we wallow in our comfort about brown children in concentration camps and brown women being sterilized by our government.

Are you starting to get the picture of what this is really about? I sure hope so. We, meaning the United States, need to get wiser as we get older. May we all begin to heal and see our worth, so that we can pass THAT along to our children.

What could I build with this life of mine if all of me was lovingly supported by the world around me?

I would build a world where we all believed that we, as humans, can be so much more. More in the sense of inner potential coming forward and into the world. The magic that we were cultivating when we were more connected to this planet and all its wonders, is not gone. We have been forced, and/or have willingly gone down a path that doesn't support us evolving into our biggest, fullest, and brightest. I feel in my heart of hearts that if ALL of me was lovingly supported, that I could be telepathic, heal myself and others, focus my energy to connect across the Universe with other beings and see how they live their lives. Far-fetched you say? A bit cray cray? Is it though, really? We don't know, because we have yet to allow it to happen. I will stand strong, honoring all the parts that make me my authentic self.

two

unapologetically ~~black~~, ~~gay~~, ~~male~~, ~~human~~ ... me

Lights swirling around my aura
Bass shaking my liver
Arms glistening with sweat
Shirt off and tucked into my back belt loop
I am shaping time around me
Bending
Grooving
Dancing
My body is electrified with the other bodies
Plugged into a synchronicity
A synchronicity that is dancing
Moving
Living
Breathing
Loving
My body

This memory brings me both joy and sadness. The memory is from more than twenty years ago. Wow, twenty years …

A bit of extra weight swirling around my waist
Alcohol pickling my liver
Arms flapping a bit when I sweat
Shirt off?!? Are you out of your mind?!?!?

I am running out of time
Bent over
Soothing
Dancing?
My body is horrified with what it is now
Plugged into a memory
A memory that was healthy
Moving
Living
Breathing
Loving?
My body

This poem is a reminder that only I get to define ME. Allowing myself the grace to be my authentic self without apology. Yes, I have gained some weight since twenty years ago, and when I read this poem again, just a few years after I wrote it, I am standing strong in my authenticity. I know that society places labels upon me, and some of those labels unleash people's prejudices, including mine. When do we finally say enough is enough? I am Black. I am gay. I am male. AND … I am human. I am ME. Unapologetically ME. The difference from then to now is that I have been decolonizing myself and detaching from the status quo. If we want true belonging for ourselves and everyone, then we have to start here, with self-recognition of the beautiful power we were each born with.

I first recognized the *light*, (I define light as the power we are born with, just by being human; it's a recognition of that power in everyone else, as well) inside of me around the age of six. I realized that the world around me thought I was funny. I could sing and dance, make silly sounds, have quick comebacks, and make everyone laugh. I was a bringer of joy.

My oldest sister, who is eight years older than me, invited some friends over. They were listening to disco songs on her eight-track player. I kept peeking at them from around the corner, waiting patiently for someone to notice me. Someone finally did, and that was all I needed to sashay my six-year-old self right into her room. I

unapologetically ~~black~~, ~~gay~~, ~~male~~, ~~human~~… ME

was dancing in no time.

"Melinda, he is such a good dancer!"

"Look at how cute he is!"

Instead of being the usual older sister, wanting to keep her friends to herself, she grabbed my pudgy little arm to bring me closer and put her rainbow-toe socks on me. These toe socks basically came up to my armpits. The room burst into laughter. My sister went to the cassette player and switched out what was playing for a new song. For *my* song. Swirling, psychedelic pulses, with a bit of outer space thrown in for good measure, blared from the speaker. I began to twirl in slow motion at first, and then the beat dropped. IT. WAS. ON.

Invitation: I hope you are familiar with Amii Stewart's cover of Eddie Floyd's 1966 classic, Knock on Wood!! If you are not, stop reading, search for it online, and listen to it, RIGHT NOW.

I was jumping, gyrating, strutting, twirling, dancing my chubby little rainbow clad legs off! Sister's friends were laughing, clapping, and smiling, and my sister was too! My mom came around the corner, saw me, laughed out loud, then pulled it together enough to tell us, "Turn it down! Your dad is sleeping. He has to work tonight!" She winked at me as she left the room. Inner light, GLOWING.

As my cognitive brain grew, I began to use this "light" to mask my own pain instead of using it to meet my own fears head-on.

"N*****! You are just a N*****!" came whipping outta their mouth. *Just make 'em laugh, Matthew. Don't engage with this ignorant* *bullshit. Just make 'em laugh.*

"I don't know why you have to call me that. We were just laughing a second ago. Can't we go back to that?" The answer, every time, was no.

Then the fighting would start. People around, almost always cheering on the one who called me the n-word and me punching as hard and as much as I could. Then, the fight would break up, the visit to the principal's office would happen, and the next day, like clockwork, I would always make 'em laugh.

I even tried to make my father laugh, just a few times. His beatings transported me to a place of darkness so profound it seemed as if I was being punished for his faults too.

It was hard to shine my light around him. It was as if the two of us were connected. Connected not only by the fact that he was my biological father, but also by the fact that he and I were each desperately trying to figure ourselves out. Connected because he never truly got the time and space for himself to do just that, and I, unknowingly, inherited all of that cellularly. This pulled my light into itself, imploding at times like a supernova. Dark moods, lashing out in anger, desiring to be alone, while also feeling debilitating pangs of loneliness. Later on in life, I'd realize that through every lash of the whip, strike of his hand, shake of my shoulders, I was absorbing all of his inability to deal with/do his own personal Work.

Invitation: Please take a moment and take a sip of water.

Revisiting the coming out story of a twelve-year-old me, fishing along the Rum River with my friend: "I think I have a crush on your older brother?" Response, "I think that is just a phase. You'll get over it." My father said the same thing years later, in his only attempt to have a conversation with me about my sexuality. I didn't learn much about my father. Between the abuse, my trying not to be around because of it, his work schedule, my moving out the day I graduated from high school, and my just plain never asking my father anything about himself. To this day, I don't really know him. I don't even have one story from him that could help me piece together why he beat me the way he did, and not his other five children. Why did he choose to only say those same words that my twelve-year-old friend once said, and then never talk to me about my love for other men? I realized several years after his passing that I learned nothing about me from him, except how I never wanted to make someone else feel shame the way he made me feel shame.

I realized that there never was "the talk" about how to deal with racist remarks, systems, and society. I wasn't told how to be a Black man, or even told stories of how it was for him to be a Black man. I once came home from floating down the river with the church youth group, and I had a couple of hickies on my neck. My dad was drunk. He smiled and laughed about it, but the laughter came from a place of pride. That's the closest we came to any kind of sex talk, or talk about the opposite sex, but I didn't need *that* talk. I would have much rather heard about my attraction to other males. Like I said already, I really don't know my own father. When I ask my siblings, they can tell me bits and pieces about my father growing up, but no real stories that could allude to what type of life he lived.

Closer to the end of his life, the first time being a day after my thirtieth birthday, he and I were alone at our cabin up north. Everyone else had gone home, and we had just gotten in from fishing. I'd caught an almost eight-pound largemouth bass. I cleaned it and he cooked it, pretty much in silence. That was our way of being in each other's company. Just being, no talking. Then he said, "I think I am the reason that you and your brother are gay." That statement opened something up inside of me that I didn't feel capable of witnessing. He was trying to come out to me. The thought slowly went through my mind, as I made sure I was comprehending clearly.

"Nah, Dad. I am gay because this is how my soul chose to be." And with that I walked outside and smoked several cigarettes until he poked his head out and said good night. I didn't tell anyone.

Then on my thirty-fourth birthday, my gay-identified brother and I were at the hospital bathing and shaving our father because he wouldn't let the female nurses do it. The one male nurse was off for the weekend. My brother had left the room, and my father said it again. "I think I am the reason that you and your brother are gay."

Again I said, "No, Dad, you aren't the reason. There is no 'reason.' It is merely the truth." He died the next day. I didn't tell anyone, not even my mom.

My mom, though …

I was home visiting a few years after Dad died. I was sitting at the kitchen table, rolling a cigarette, when my mom brought out this book, *On the Down Low: A Journey into the Lives of Straight Black Men Who Sleep with Men* written by J. L. King and Karen Hunter[3]. She set it in front of me and said, "Your brother showed me this book. I have read it, and I think this was your father. All those times I thought he was cheating on me with a woman, I think it was actually a man." I couldn't tell her about the two times that I couldn't be there for her husband, my father, when he was trying to come out to me. I just didn't have the tools necessary to deal with that and his physical and emotional abuse. It was too much. Everything that fuels my Shadow side was apparent to me at that moment. I wasn't able to recognize that until years later. I felt the pressure of needing to be something that I was not, my father's definition of who I was supposed to be, a good son. I get to define ME, no one else. Authentically ME.

What did you learn or internalize from a parent, authority figure, or someone you looked up to? How has it shaped who you are? How has it shaped your thoughts? Do you have a personal expectation to "live up" to? Someone else's ideas of you? Of life? Of success? Take a moment, or two, and write out your lived experiences around these questions.

I feel as if there's a part of me that has always known that I am the light. My parents were God-fearing people, so we kids had to go to church. I was devoted. I often went and spent a lot of time at the church, thinking the abuse at home would let up if I just got closer to God. How the sexual thoughts of other males would just go away if I just got closer to God. Now, I see how internalized racial oppressions and internalized homophobia played a large part in this, but I will save that for another chapter. We will stick to the light.

When I traveled abroad for the first time at the age of fifteen, a woman at a church in Scotland locked eyes with me. She walked across the room with her walker, took my hand, and began to speak tongues to me. I smiled nervously and when she finished, I shakily said, "I am sorry. I don't speak in tongues, nor do I understand it." She smiled and replied, "You don't need to know what I said. Just know that you will be someone of importance one day." Fifteen years old, a child of abuse, a magnet for people to come to and be made happy by my jovial and easy ways. Of course, this moment was pivotal to me! No one else, before that moment, took the time to really see me, and from her gaze, words, stature, I knew she SAW me. I can honestly say that it was one of the moments that I actually saw ME, as well. Pivotal. Maybe there was something inside me that was yearning to be set free, liberated if you will. I tucked this moment and all of its feelings away, hid them behind what I was internalizing about myself, and my worth. It would be years before I would look back and truly see this moment for the start it was, because I might have hidden them but the light it was giving off couldn't be fully blocked.

Please share a pivotal point in your life when you felt liberated by a choice that you made for yourself.

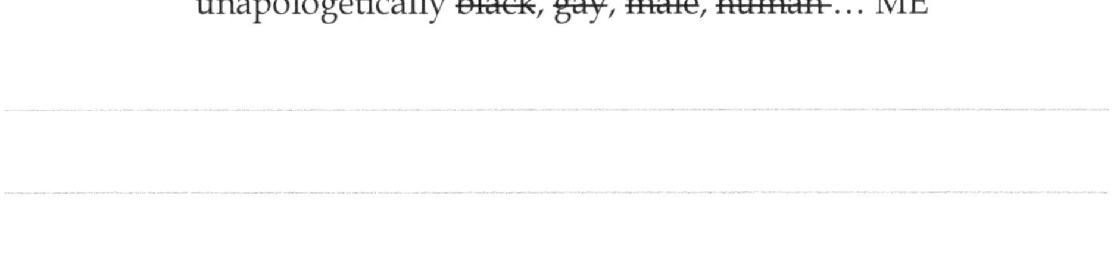

My lived experiences have brought me to the conclusion that we all are someone of importance. I strongly believe that what I tapped into that day in Scotland was what we all, as human beings, have inside of us. A desire to want to learn, grow, and expand outwards, just like the Universe is doing every moment of every day. We all deserve to let our light shine to its biggest, fullest, and brightest. I feel it shines brightest when we have a balance of mind, body, and spirit. This is the base structure of a triality perspective. A perspective where lived experience takes us off of the status quo binary to places our lived experience expands beyond the status quo box.

The triality perspective allows the expansion of humanity, instead of the duality or binary that the dominant white culture has us believing. This binary confines humanity between two points. It is easier for the status quo to leverage the "divide and conquer" method if it keeps humans believing that there are only two options to choose from in any given situation; right-wrong, good-bad, black-white. Even the gray in between the two points is tarnished with complacency and stunted growth. The status quo gets its power from relying on us to strive for comfort, and this comfort comes from our complacency. If we stay within the two points, allowing the gray to lead us, then we strive for comfort instead of the growth of humanity.

An example of the dangers of duality perspective is the status quo driven response that not all cops (teachers, actors, fill-in-the-blank with a person who has perceived power) are bad. "There are only a few bad apples." This response has stunted any and all attempts of rebuilding and/or asking more of those who have power.

This became apparent in my life watching educators who said

they wanted to build a new school; who said they wanted to step outside of the boxes, but could only step out as far as their lived experiences would allow them. Therefore, they would hold onto outdated ideas that were hurtful and harmful, especially to our marginalized students. For example, we built a new school, but kept grading and discipline systems that were rooted in white cisgendered supremacy culture. For that matter, structuring our "new school" within these same parameters of supremacy culture.

Looking at the triality perspective, one in which the third point, YOU, can allow your creativity, imagination, determination, execution to expand and place your dot/choice/perspective out into the Universe for transformation allowing humanity to also expand into its biggest, fullest, and brightest No longer do we say either, or. Now, we can say either, or, AND. Like I said, we all have light within us, what matters is how we choose to shine it.

Words my therapists have said to me, advice given by friends, by my lovers, by my chosen family, and read in the pages of Brené Brown: they are my education.

"My past is my education. My future is my inspiration. My present is my creation."[4] When I first read these three sentences from *Medicine Cards, Revised Expanded Edition* by Jamie Sams and David Carson, a tarot deck I use during my morning meditations, it all locked right in. My light is shining on seven generations past, which is my education, and on seven generations to the future, which is my inspiration. I used to think of a past situation, or be triggered by something in the moment of a conversation, and instantly be whisked back in time to a place of hurt and shame. I would not be able to get myself out of it; I was too ashamed of many aspects of me. My internalized oppressions would have me shrink back from just allowing myself to BE.

Once I let myself learn from my lived experiences, I began to actively listen to others. I recognized when I was sabotaging myself from simply just being. I began taking these newly found ways of viewing myself and my presence in the world, and I began trying a multitude of healing, learning, and spiritual practices. I was building my toolbox of self-awareness. This didn't just happen overnight. This took time. Mainly because of how deeply entrenched those first abusive episodes were and when they occurred in my cognitive upbringing. I am learning how to allow myself grace. If you can relate to any of this, I ask that you learn from it and allow yourself to grow. If you don't see what it is you are learning at that moment, let it go. The lesson will come back again with a different name and face. YES! *The past is my education.*

The future is my inspiration, because I want better for humanity, not just for myself. All these realizations allowed me to see the third sentence: *The present is my creation.* I must now build an example, for generations to come, of what it means to nurture humanity into growth. I/we are/ am creation. We are our ancestors' seventh generation.

I am shining my light on what it means to lead with humanity. This "leading with humanity" was not always clearly laid out for me. It is important for us all to know that we are more than the identifiers we place upon ourselves, and that others place upon us. Being unapologetic about our authenticity is necessary for humanity to evolve. This is why it is important for us to understand that we should give away (invest) money, knowledge, and unconditional love to help guide others to their understanding of their light that is shining.

My light was dimmed. It was dimmed because of the beatings and gaslighting and what I believed about what the status quo had ingrained into me about its "value" of the almighty dollar. Status quo has been telling me since I was a child that I need to amass wealth in order to have any dignity or sense of worth for myself. As a child, there were times when we did not have food. I grew up being told that if you don't have the money for it then you weren't supposed to have it, that God was looking out for us and ensuring we weren't spending our money sinfully. Status quo indoctrinated me into thinking I needed to ensure that I was spending money on items that were truly needed, and not on wants. The trap I fell prey to was that the status quo defined what was needed. So, I looked outside for approval on what I could spend money on and what I couldn't. Status quo traps us all into looking outside of ourselves instead of listening to ourselves. Does that lesson, fueled by the status quo's construct, really come into play when your father has lung cancer and the doctor bills pile up?

The past is your education. Here is where the rubber meets the road. I have been trying to hold onto this idea that wealth equates evil. I was born poor, raised poor, a starving artist, and funded my programs while I taught. Now, here I am. Rich in friends, experiences, empathy, love, and much more. My pocketbook is still, by others' standards, poor, yet my *light*, my HUMANITY, is shining brighter than it ever has. If I had continued down the path of what value the status quo puts on money, its ideas of success, and/or who it claims has power, I wouldn't be sitting here typing this for you to read. Status quo urges us all that every moment needs to be productive. Instead, I would be working eighty-two hours a week just to claim my worth in this existence.

Take a moment to share your lived experiences around these ideas of power. I used money as an example of the status quo ideas of power. How do you define power? Who have you given your power to? What has happened to get you to come to these conclusions? Please share your thoughts.

unapologetically ~~black~~, ~~gay~~, ~~male~~, ~~human~~… ME

All of the moments throughout my life have led me to where I am now:

- Becoming a theater major, marching in drum corps
- Taking dance classes
- Teaching winter guard
- Moving to Chicago to perform
- Moving to Seattle
- All my jobs and performances in Seattle
- Being a Risk of Change Giant Puppets Mask and Mummery troupe member
- Moving to Amsterdam
- Moving back to Seattle
- Working at UPS
- Managing apartments
- Becoming a licensed educator
- Moving to Southern Oregon
- Creating a school with other educators
- Building a public school theater and dance program
- Resigning from teaching
- Going to Charlottesville
- Working with the Racial Equity Coalition
- Conducting Race Toolkit talks
- Igniting Matthew Reynolds Consulting, LLC
- Meeting and working with Trena Bolden Fields, my coach and marketing mentor
- Working with my first therapist of color
- Moving to Volcano, Hawai'i

These were all moments of clarity. All of these moments are filled with life. Each one pulled me forward to this moment, allowing myself to learn and grow, allowing myself to heal. So many sights and sounds, smells and tastes, always feeling there was more life to live. Moving deeper into clarity is using the knowledge that I am worthy. This is not a passing phase. I am fully present in this moment. My authentic self knows it is worthy and it is leading me forward. These moments are lasting longer and longer before my Shadow side interrupts. I then remember that I am to be loved, and to be love.

I will repeat this again later: at my best, the emotions I am feeling have their time, and move on. Nothing gets "stuck." I don't shrink back from the emotions that are coming up. I also put no attachment on them, such as good or bad, right or wrong. Therefore, no guilt or shame is allowed to take hold of me. I just allow myself the feelings. This is worth repeating over and over.

The little boy in me is healing. He is growing up. I deserve to BE. In this moment, I deserve to say who I want to work with and why I want to work with them. No more dragging myself toward the status quo's ideas of success. If I am giving myself grace, and grace to others, I have come to the conclusion that I am not for everyone. I am not willing to allow others' inability to desire learning to harm me emotionally, physically, and/or spiritually; boundaries. The status quo tries to shoehorn humanity into the same box, the same ideas of success, power, and worthiness. Giving myself grace means that I am allowing my authentic self to become fully realized, here and now. Knowing that the status quo cannot take that away from me, or anyone else. We are all on our journey, and that path is for the individual, NOT the status quo. I will also say that we are all human, and humanity's journey is unapologetic in its need for growth.

Throughout my life, I have had to come to terms with the fact that I AM WORTHY. That humanity is worthy of so much more than what the dominant culture has taught us. That I (and you, and everyone you meet) should be celebrated for being Unapologetically ME. Just as there are a plethora of stars in the galaxy, I have many more realizations in this lifetime and this chapter could continue for a length of time. I am so much more than the identifiers that I place upon myself, and/or that society places upon me. That is why I peel back each of those identifiers so that I can get to the core of ME. Unapologetically ME.

I have a responsibility to my ancestors, my education, and a responsibility to seven generations from now, my inspiration. These are tools I want to leave for the next generations, so that the lifting they have to do isn't so heavy, cumbersome, and debilitating. It is important to my Work, my heart, my world, that I acknowledge what has come before me and what is to come after me. I am modeling this for everyone that is around me on a daily basis.

Invitation: Take a moment to turn on your current favorite song, one that makes you want to MOVE. Then take the time to dance/sway/move to this song.

integrity vs. loyalty

So. Fucking. Tired.
Clenched Jaw
Hot tears
Knotted stomach
More death and dying, this time in the name of blue lives

Seventeen years old
Wanting to be
A police officer
They need my help
Take my gun, my AR-15
Run
Run to help
Kill those who oppose
My brothers and sisters in blue

I feel their blood
Before hearing about it
I feel their blood
Knotted in my stomach
I am cast into my past

Remembering gut wrenching dreams
of a seventeen-year-old white-bodied male
shooting all my students
running out of bullets when it is my turn to be killed

I resigned from teaching after having the dream described in the poem for the third time. I couldn't allow myself to be a part of the US education system because it is harmful to students.

The district I worked at had an aggressive stance for me to be loyal to their ideas, many of which were hurtful and harmful to our Black, Indigenous, and People of Color (BIPoC) students, and therefore to ALL of our students. Loyalty, when used to manipulate, coerce, and leverage is nothing good for humanity.

Every day I see the idea of being loyal. From social media posts to conversations with friends and family to eavesdropping in the grocery store check-out line, I hear whispers of things like:

"Why don't you go along with my post/tweet/ meme?"

"YOU always have to contradict what I say!"

"Did you fact check it?"

"Don't you trust me?"

"Don't you see me as a friend?"

"If you were loyal to our friendship you would just go along with it in public, and then we could talk about it in private as friends, because that's what friends do. Friends are loyal to one another, no matter what!"

Wow, even just typing that all out was taxing on my soul. I try my best to live my life with integrity to who I am, Unapologetically ME. If someone else wants me to put me aside just to be loyal to them, fuck that!

If I am loyal to an identifier, an identity that I use to explain aspects of my being, and someone makes an ignorant statement against that identifier, and others who also use that identifier "cancel" the person who made the ignorant statement, then it is almost demanded that I am to be loyal to the rest and follow suit, thus canceling that person, as well.

Now, I might have never had a conversation with that person and, therefore, no connection to be able to sit them down and have a conversation about how hurtful, harmful, and hateful their statement was. This would allow them an opportunity to see my humanity, and I to see theirs. Instead, this quick decision is made to "cancel" the other person. Also, many of these situations happen to those in a position of power, someone who I would have absolutely no connection with. It all stays at such a distance that it makes it almost impossible to truly experience each other's humanity.

If I stay in integrity to my truth, allowing myself to be who I am, then I am giving my humanity an opportunity, at least, to lead. Now if someone is coming at me aggressively, wishing harm, or screaming hateful profanities at myself and others who might share the same identifier, then no, I won't engage. I also won't "cancel" them out. I know what that feels like up against my soul. It doesn't feel like what we as humans are supposed to be doing with one another.

I see the idea of cancel culture coming from the same place that perfectionism comes from when white supremacy culture speaks of its "pure" blood lines. Demanding only perfection doesn't allow for humanity to be more, to grow into something. White cisgendered supremacy culture limits the growth of humanity. White-bodied supremacy wants your loyalty to embody it and only it. If I "cancel" a person for their comments, how will humanity grow?

The current status quo, which is immersed in white cisgendered supremacy culture, doesn't allow us to have more sides and stories. Divide and conquer doesn't work when there are multiple sides and when we take the time to actually listen to each other's stories.

Having said that, it seems that since Black and Brown-bodied folx started using the word cancel to hold people accountable on Twitter, white cisgendered supremacy culture has co-opted and repeated cancel culture. Now, it has taken on an entirely different slant. White cisgendered supremacy culture continues to weaponize the slang of underserved groups and use it back on them with the childish sentiment of, "If you're gonna cancel me, then I'm gonna cancel you!" It is, yet again, pointing a finger toward something I just don't think supports the multi-faceted depths of a human. I also believe cancel culture, when weaponized, can be dehumanizing, demoralizing, and a powerful tool of white-bodied supremacy.

If I "cancel" a person, I might never be able to sit down and have a conversation with that person about how hurtful, harmful, and hateful their statement was, therefore allowing them an opportunity to see my humanity, and I to see theirs. Instead, this quick decision is made to "cancel" the other person in the name of loyalty to the community of one of my identifiers. Canceling often happens to those in a position of power, like celebrities, authors, or politicians. People who I would have absolutely no connection with. It all stays at such a distance that it's almost impossible to truly experience each other's humanity.

Invitation: Gentle reminder to drink some water.

I wasn't always living with integrity to myself and my ideas. When I was hired at the school district where I taught, I believed that we would be building a brand new school system, with new ideas and approaches to education. Teaching the whole child, holding ourselves and our students accountable to these new ideals, and moving the needle forward for the education system nationally was, in my original understanding, the focus. We started in that direction, some will even say we achieved what I just wrote, yet it fell short of dismantling the old ways entrenched into the system. It remained loyal, knowingly and unknowingly, to the ideas of indoctrination that continue to lead the US educational system. Indoctrination into the white-bodied supremacy, hierarchal, patriarchal, capitalistic system.

I remember sitting in a professional development meeting and realizing that all the books that we had read so far had been written by cisgendered white males or females. There was nothing that we had read so far that represented the makeup of our society. Instead, it was showing me that the only people who could come up with new formulas, new scientific/psychological concepts, discovery of other people, creation of poetic forms could only be white-bodied cisgendered heterosexual abled people (mostly male).

Because of my lived experiences, self-worth, and internalized racial oppressions, I listened when I was told to not rock the boat, have empathy for others' stories, and keep my name off because some won't follow if my name is on it. I was loyal to these thoughts of me, and what I was bringing to a table that I started feeling more and more like I wasn't truly invited to. I didn't speak up about my lived experiences as, for a long time, I was the only licensed employee of color in the entire school district. This is how I knew what the students in our small BIPoC student body were going through. I saw in them what I had experienced as a youth in my predominantly white upbringing in central Minnesota. Growing up in school, there was no representation–Black or gay, there were continual aggressions in the hallway, racial and homophobic slurs, and a surprising number of educators uncomfortable addressing these issues when affected students brought it to them. It was decades later, and the same shit was going on for my students. I just couldn't believe it, so I chose to keep quiet, fortress myself in the theater, not talk for years in professional development meetings, and show them I was loyal to what "we" were building.

"I am in the system, I can change it from within," I thought. No. It needs folx fighting outside of the system. Within it, they've got you. They know that you will do anything for your students, and while you are busy fighting for your students, you get pulled away from the larger picture of REBUILDING the system. When I saw the actual qualitative information that showed the metrics of how we were failing our students of color, and people still chose to say I was wrong, I could no longer jeopardize my integrity and reconcile that which they thought was going wrong with my own humanity.

Staying within integrity with my humanity means taking action that supports my truth. On a cellular level, I feel stunted by the status quo, socialization, and the construct of whiteness being the "dominant" culture. Some have said, "Don't give it any power over you! You are stronger than that! How can you blame all your problems on just that one thing, really?"

My response is: Tell me, what else is at the root of the status quo? Dominant culture is not just one thing anymore; it has tendrils that spread out and into our concepts of self, government systems, faith, and spirituality. We are supposed to be loyal to it, not question it, and work to uphold it.

My responsibility is to my truth, to my authentic self. I'm responsible for showing how to uproot indoctrination and brainwashing that has occurred to make a few wealthy and feel that they have power over me and others. Think about how much stronger and more vibrant, magical, and loving we humans could be if we allowed ourselves to empower our connection to each other and everything else on this planet.

I see this idea of "loyalism" entrenched in nationalism, brotherhood, religion, capitalism, and so forth. What about integrity? Why can't we be loyal to THAT idea? According to the Oxford Dictionary[5], integrity is the quality of being honest and having strong moral principles; moral uprightness. What would you do if you were asked to "just not tell the truth," but to stay loyal to those who might be protected by not saying anything? Write about what you would do.

As I sit here typing this out, I am realizing that integrity above loyalty is what allows me to go beyond the limitations of the status quo. Indoctrination into any culture can limit an individual's potential, especially if that culture has expectations of loyalty to them, instead of integrity with oneself.

Awww, I see your furrowed brow. Let me explain this more.

If I choose to be loyal to a friend, even though I know the secret they are asking me to keep is harmful to them, am I truly a friend? If I stay within integrity to myself, I will instead tell the friend that what they are doing is harmful to their own health. I can then help them myself, and/or get them the help they need. Loyalty limits full expression of self because you are always having to look outside of yourself in order to take into consideration what others will think of your choices/decisions. Being in integrity with yourself you start with looking inside (your instincts) to see what you need/want/desire in order to make your choices/decisions. Basically–stop looking out and start looking in.

The world around you will not know that it isn't allowing you to fully be you unless you tell it such. My mama always said, "Closed mouth doesn't get fed." Standing up for your own ideas, knowing that it doesn't matter if others believe you, and respecting others when they stand up for their ideas, is key to crafting a world of full potential, belonging, and unconditional love. Yes, there are people out there who want to tear other people down. It makes them feel … something. For the most part though, others who we wish to blame for us not asking for what we want/need, do not wake up and think, "You know what, I am going to mess up Pat's day today, just because I can." Get over yourself. Most of the time, others really, truly aren't thinking of us in this way. Keep moving forward.

Now, don't get this confused with what I said before. I feel that it is important for us to trust our instincts and our lived experiences. The dominant culture has used gaslighting to make people constantly question their own sanity. The dominant culture gaslights to help leverage the divide and conquer tactic and to keep us from trusting our own instincts. This makes me think of a person who I passed in the hallway and said "good morning" to every day for ten years. EVERY SINGLE DAY. Not once did they EVER reply. People told me that maybe they didn't hear me, or maybe they were thinking about something else. I told myself that it wasn't because they were racist, homophobic, and/or didn't like me. I was assimilating to the ideas of professionalism being loyal to the gaslighting of others making excuses for this colleague's non-response. Instead, I needed to trust my instincts and to be in integrity with myself. This is very different from standing up for your own ideas.

"Assimilationists are people who like you, but only with quotation marks. Like … 'like' you. Meaning, they 'like' you because you're like them."[6]

If I were to fully assimilate to the situation and never say good morning again, I wouldn't have been in integrity with my instincts; which invite me to be kind to those around me. Assimilation at times has meant survival, and being within integrity means I am living my life authentically.

Take a moment, write down what feelings, thoughts, emotions, lived experiences are coming up for you after reading the last piece. Please share.

I am not here to feed these things to you because I don't know your lived experiences. Were you a part of a school that was diverse, taught about the Bacon Rebellion, showed diverse examples of genius or were some of your experiences similar to mine? When thinking about your lived experiences and the things that you've been indoctrinated into, those will be different from mine. Throughout this book, your Work will be to look at those lessons that you had throughout your life. I hope you choose the discomfort of unlearning the half-truths and lies of this nation, so that you may create room to learn the truth by living within *your* integrity. And with that truth, I hope we build something that is beneficial for ALL to be their biggest, fullest, and brightest.

Loyalty Limits Full Expression!

You have me say a pledge to a piece of fabric
You have me sing an anthem that is racist in its very nature

You have me leave aspects of me at the door
You have me do all of this so that I am
LOYAL to the dream
LOYAL to the Amerikkkan dream
LOYAL to anything/anyone
but to myself

four

F.A.I.L. (first attempt in learning)

The young think that failure is the Siberian end of the line, banishment from all the living, and tend to do what I then did–which was to hide.
– James Baldwin[7]

Achievement, THEN you belong
Achievement, then YOU belong
Achievement, then you BELONG
This is part of the indoctrination
The indoctrination into this nation
The ideas we keep uplifting, striving toward
This is the meat and potatoes of the status quo
Don't believe me? Look at your own education and what you value now
See, now whatcha gonna do, now that you know?

Perfectionism, the deep root of the status quo, is something that feeds shame for so many of us. If it isn't perfect then there's something wrong with me. This also has a tendency to lend itself to how we define success. As we attempt something new, experience something different from our norm, or just go into the world wanting a change, these Shadow dwellers called perfectionism and success keep us from the rich, fertile learning that comes from failing. We don't take our time to self-reflect on what it was that kept us from achieving, and what kept us coming back again and again until we learned what it was we were after. As Baldwin says, we hide. Hiding from ourselves makes us not want to be seen as a failure by those who uphold these ideas of perfectionism, or project their definitions of success upon us. WE ARE WORTHY ENOUGH TO FAIL! That's where the real learning begins.

Dig into that learning.

I remember when I first started color guard, there was a particular toss called a helicopter. This was super scary, because the idea was to toss the flag above your head in a way that made it rotate parallel to the ground, like a helicopter blade. Then, as it came down, rotating, you caught it as it wrapped around your face and into your waiting hands in front of your eyes, while keeping your feet planted in the same spot. I tossed HUNDREDS of helicopters, with much swearing, before I even started to catch them, let alone catch them parallel to the ground. The payoff was the crowds cheering and screaming when we, as a team, tossed flags rotating at the same height and speed, to be caught by each and every one of us in unison. I would have never gotten to that point if I hadn't experienced failure and then had someone watching, coaching, supporting me at every toss. "A little more rotation! Flick the wrist more! Release higher! Release lower!" Keep trying, because with every failure you are growing stronger.

Don't duck and hide from it. Stand strong, feet planted, and try again, and again, and again. James Baldwin didn't want to hide, I believe. It was a survival technique. If all the systems around you are telling you that achievement is what you must do FIRST, and THEN you can belong, while at the same time you have a system telling you that you don't belong because of your identifiers, what is one to do? Hide. James Baldwin moved away from those he loved. He watched as our government assassinated Malcolm X, Martin Luther King Jr., and after he left, Fred Hampton. Hiding became survival. James, you did what you needed to do, and that has helped me and so many others stand strong. For that, I am grateful.

Standing strong in the face of a culture that takes away your humanity in so many different ways, even down to the very idea of failing, is the strength that my ancestors, such as James Baldwin, have given me. James Baldwin survived to give us more tools through his writing. This is similar to the tools that I am helping others to craft and crafting myself, to then leave behind for the next generations to pick up, swing, chop, carve, and craft their way into belonging. Thank you, ancestors.

When have you felt that you failed and then hid? How did that serve you? What was at risk that made you hide? When looking back, knowing what you do now, how might have you stood strong? What might you have gained from reflecting on your attempts as they came? Take a moment now, and write.

Fail is something, according to my father's wrath, I did ALL. THE. TIME. There was nothing that I could do "right," and therefore, I was a failure. Growing up, I saw how indoctrination into the world of shame was leading my life. I didn't know how to get myself up and out of the beaten into submission perfectionism that was happening. It all had to be right. It all had to happen in order. It all needed to be perfect. But it wasn't, nor is life supposed to be. I was missing all of the rich, fertile soil that is found within the FAIL.

If I had allowed myself to look around during those points of imperfection, I might have seen how those moments were helping me to get to a sense of belonging. Let me explain. When those moments of failure were happening, this cloak of shame would be drawn up and over me, keeping me from seeing others around me who were also not achieving the task at hand. A flag toss, math problem, dance move, memorization of lines in a play; I would be so focused that I didn't see others struggle, let alone ask for help. This all began to shift once I found myself going through the Master of Arts in Teaching (MAT) program at Southern Oregon University.

In the program, many of the stories I am sharing with you here were flooding my memories. The main takeaway was that I did not want to project on my future students all this bullshit I had unknowingly inherited during my cognitive development and beyond. I wanted to make sure that my students were allowed to fail, look at how they got there, and figure out how to get themselves out of it without shaming themselves into oblivion. The language landed smack in my face when a colleague used the term F.A.I.L. First Attempt In Learning.

Life changer! Not only was I supporting all of my students with this new way of exploring their "failures," but I was also healing from a lot of my past shame. By allowing myself to F.A.I.L., looking deeply, and reflecting on how I got there, I began to love myself more and more. I began to not only believe in belonging, but I was living it by allowing myself to belong. Allowing my authentic self to be a part of the world I occupied. Referring to the helicopter toss story from before, I didn't just shut out my instructors' and teammates' voices. I listened and adjusted my tosses so that I could truly feel, in my body, what it was like to do a great toss. To not only do it once, but to replicate that great toss again and again. As some know, it goes beyond that in the color guard world. Not only are you replicating that great toss, but you are also feeling the energy being given off by ALL of your teammates, so that you ALL toss in unison. That can't happen if you are stuck in a shame spiral, being led by only the ideas of achievement and perfectionism. It has to be led by knowing, feeling, and believing that you are where you belong.

When I look at the state of our country, extremely divisive with that division being leveraged every chance that folx get, I can't help but look at this concept of F.A.I.L. If you aren't holding up nationalism, patriotism, white cisgendered supremacy culture, then you are a failure. WE as a nation, won't allow ourselves to F.A.I.L.

More and more of the truth of what we, as a nation, have done to our Indigenous people, to the original stewards of this land is being revealed. WE, the USA, killed them by disease, starvation, marched them for miles on the Trail of Tears, killed their food source, killed their women and children, and continue to this day. ALL of this is still happening. As this truth is coming out through research and educating oneself and/or people searching for it; other people are fighting equally hard for this truth to be silenced, for a multitude of reasons. One reason, I feel, is because WE, in the USA, are not allowed to be anything but the white cisgendered supremacy culture. We have been fed this notion from the beginning of this nation, and through our athletes, soldiers, education systems, monetary wealth, resources, and so forth., we try to reinforce that WE ARE THE BEST!

We aren't the best though. More of us are seeing that and more of us are deeply FEELING that. What could we become if we, as a nation, acknowledge that we are still learning? How could we advance humanity if we just said, "Well, that was a failure. What did we learn? How can we grow? What will it become?" Instead, at a dizzying pace, we cover everything up and shout really loudly, "USA! USA! USA!" while out the other side of our mouths, we say, "Don't look behind that curtain." Can we please just STOP.

Invitation: Inhale-2-3-4-5-6-7-hold-4-3-2-1-exhale-6-5-4-3-2-1. Repeat three more times.

Now, what did you just learn? Take a moment to self-reflect and write it out. This is a tool to be utilized when that shame spiral starts to swirl around you, when failure is imminent. Breathe the moment in. Regroup. Look around. Learn from it. Grow, because we all deserve to belong.

Through my lived experiences, and as a youth in my father's home, is when the ideas of being perfect came before my feeling of belonging. The education system picked it up from there, saying that for me to belong, I must achieve on a level that fits their criteria of what makes a "good" student. That still holds true in our education system, even though Maslow's Hierarchy of Needs (which originated from the Blackfoot Nation[8]) says that a sense of belonging needs to come before achievement.

The current backbone of our education system indoctrinates us into the ideas of achievement. In our education system, we are reinforcing that you must achieve before you can belong, completely skipping all the strength, perseverance, grit, determination, that comes from F.A.I.L. The education system was designed like a factory. Pushing, pulling, and yanking kids through, without regard to their emotional well-being, without regard to what they are learning—just a conveyor belt that constantly moves them toward what the dominant society has deemed success looks like. Generation after generation has been indoctrinated into this belief, and this way of thinking has stunted the growth of humanity, keeping us away from our full potential.

I've seen my students not even attempt something new because the fear that this system puts into our youth, that they might fail, is palpable. It has increased their anxiety and has even increased their feelings of loneliness. The UK created a Minister of Loneliness position in 2019 because the problem had become so prevalent in the youth there. While here in the US, we continue with the facade that there isn't anything wrong, thus burying any studies that go against that perfectionist idea. We are failing our youth, because we refuse to admit failure.

The status quo loves to watch car crashes, failures, and mistakes happen. Time and time again, headlines are filled with evidence of these failures. Even if there is success, it is often overshadowed by previous failures. This is seen through "canceling" of people, and also with our prison system. The dualism of either you fail or you succeed leads to the inability to recover from mistakes (F.A.I.L.s).

When people make bigger mistakes that are against the law and end up serving time in prison, the dominant culture says, "WE WILL NEVER FORGET OR FORGIVE." Some of these people will serve their time and then re-enter the world to become a "contributing member of society." However, they will not be able to escape those past mistakes. Instead, people who have been in prison, whether they committed a crime or not, have to fill out job applications where they are required to check the box that they are a felon. Many are stripped of their right to vote, and they are constantly judged on the fact that they were caught committing a crime. We continue to embed within our systems that failure is unacceptable to the status quo.

Not only do we continue to punish people for crimes for which they've served their time, but we also limit their ability to rediscover their path to find their biggest, fullest, and brightest selves. We are actively saying that we don't believe that people can learn from their mistakes. That they'll continue to keep making them, so we have to continue punishing them. This is the trappings of worth being tied to achievement. This allows the dominant culture to become obsessed with looking and focusing on people's mistakes. This is why F.A.I.L. can be the hardest thing to do.

The shock and surprise of failing keeps us humble and helps us to honor our First Attempt In Learning (F.A.I.L.). Rather than put us in a negative place of not deserving to be our biggest, fullest, and brightest, it brings us to a place where we can find and offer others insight, knowledge, and wisdom without expectations of recompense. Allowing ourselves to have a "growth mindset" instead of a "fixed mindset" lets us unconditionally learn "up" from a place that most would only consider a failure.

Words like determination, perseverance, and grit have F.A.I.L. as part of their foundation. Letting ourselves glean even the smallest amount of learning from an attempt, we can fuel our determination to reach a goal. F.A.I.L. will fuel your desire for accomplishment, and even if you don't make it to THE end result, you likely have fun learning along the way and maybe even forget what you first set out to achieve.

Grit and growth mindset are what we want for everyone, because it guides them to be their biggest, fullest, and brightest. Schools, parents, and society will often use the terms "grit," "growth mindset," "pull yourself up by your bootstraps," and "perseverance" to uphold a tendril of the white cisgendered supremacy culture. That is where those words and mindset are deadly. How do we build belonging first, so that all people can enjoy the journey that is F.A.I.L.?

To have a strong sense of belonging, it is important for us, as individuals, to understand our personal worth. The idea of failing and its entrenchment in the status quo feeds us lies about how our worth is tied directly to our achievements in life. The expected achievements usually look like climbing the ladder, going to college as the only pathway to a successful future, the house with the white picket fence, two point five kids, and a car in the garage. It is important to understand that it all starts with you. What is your definition of success? What is your idea of being worthy? Who are you allowing yourself to be vulnerable with, knowing that vulnerability helps you gain a sense of worth? And, how do you apply all of these answers to your sense of belonging? (Of course, knowing you will F.A.I.L. along the way.) Lastly, it is all about learning from what you find along the path of F.A.I.L.

Say you are walking down a path in the forest and looking for a way out, but then you stumble into a dead end and find blueberries … Not what you were looking for—F.A.I.L.—but now you learned something valuable. You try again … another dead end—F.A.I.L.— but now you find some strawberries, a waterfall, a swimming hole, and so forth. Still valuable, and now you know the forest better. You turn a corner, and there is the way out of the forest. Now, not only have you learned how to get through the forest, but you also know where there are blueberries, strawberries, a waterfall, and a swimming hole to enjoy during your next walk through the forest. To F.A.I.L. is to gain wisdom.

Sometimes F.A.I.L. means that you experience something

over and over again. Maybe you try to apply it a few times, but you need to go through it a few more times. Then you do this cycle over and over again before you actually start to learn, know, understand and feel that thing you were trying to learn. Growth doesn't just happen in the first, second, or even third attempt. Growth happens throughout the whole process of F.A.I.L. That's where the learning happens.

The Universe continues to grow and expand. Are we allowing ourselves to grow and expand? Are we so focused on the goals/accomplishments/medals/grades that we're ignoring what fuels us to continue to move forward? To find the things that spark our passions? "Getting out of your own way" is the epitome of F.A.I.L.

Invitation: Accountability Partner!

Accountability means building one another up through integrity, which leads us toward equity, liberation, and inclusion. Think of someone you feel belonging with—someone you feel will tell you that you are failing, help you to keep going, and inspire (motivate/encourage) you to stay true to your mission. ASK firmly, truthfully, and with loving support, if that person will become your accountability partner. Your accountability partner will help guide you through the moments when you don't see the blueberries, because you're so stuck on getting out of the forest. You will be doing this same service back.

- This partner will also be the person with whom you share your current answers to the following questions: What is *your* definition of success?

- What is *your* idea of being worthy?

- Who are you allowing yourself to be vulnerable with, knowing that vulnerability helps you gain a sense of worth?

Please remember that you are listening for discrepancies in prior truths spoken. It's important to hold the line of integrity without telling someone what they have done wrong. As you become more familiar, you may begin to recognize moments of self-sabotage/bouts of shame and guilt.

As an accountability partner, we don't want to exacerbate these moments. We want to acknowledge them for what they are so that we may grow and learn from them. One of the key factors of being a strong accountability partner is to always be actively listening. This means listening from a place of unconditional support to help uphold the other's integrity. Your ever changing answers to these questions will be the guideposts for your accountability partner to help you quiet the voices of the status quo so that F.A.I.L. can have its due process.

May we all find some blueberries, strawberries, a waterfall, and a swimming hole along the way.

lifelong learning and growth mindset

It is important to know your personal history
Don't recoil or regret, open up, face it, and embrace it

It is all you, all of it, so learn from it

From that understanding comes wisdom
This wisdom helps us to reach the furthest most shores in our
journeys

The PAST is our education

much love

Throughout history there are stories that tell of humans being used
for their labor; expendable, worthy of nothing but to make someone
else wealthy. A common thread in all these stories is that if the
masses were educated, this enslavement wouldn't be permitted.
White cisgendered supremacy culture is rooted in this story. The
capital of another human being, their labor, their very body, is meant
to be used by those who are perceived to be smarter, more powerful,
and more worthy than they, the fodder, are.

Humanity, being human, has so much more to offer than
being someone else's slave labor. Even if one never finds themself on
an academic track, being a lifelong learner means that a person

understands their innate power to learn. That learning can come from meeting new people who have a different culture, speak a different language, have a different faith, different origin story of humanity, different way of tying their shoes. Allowing each other to grow and thrive with these differences, and at times celebrating these differences, is being a lifelong learner. We were not meant to climb a ladder to someone else's definition of success. Humanity was meant to expand, just like the Universe is expanding. By allowing ourselves to continually learn, we allow ourselves to continually expand.

As we expand out, it's important to recognize, as Parker Palmer says in his book, *The Courage to Teach*, we are all "teacher, learner, knower."[9] In the course of a conversation–an hour, a day, a year–we wear these hats again and again. We switch one out for another as our capacity for growth expands into the new knowledge we're gaining as life is happening. The best example I have of this is from being in the classroom.

I'd explain something about Shakespeare to my students, and suddenly, I could tell the lightbulb went off for a couple of them. One student would raise their hand and say, "Is this what you meant?" and proceed to explain it all in their language. Then the room would light up with three or four more students who now understood the point I was making about Shakespeare. I was the teacher, and then students became the teachers as I wore the learner hat with the rest of our circle, and at the end of the conversation we all were the knower.

As I also learned from Parker Palmer, it is important to nurture the magic in your subject area by not making yourself the gatekeeper of everything that is your subject area[10]. When we create lesson plans, discuss what we find important about the subject, write up the tests, and give all of it our opinion in the form of a grade, we are gatekeeping the subject area. When we put the subject area into the middle of the circle, which is the room, then we get to witness our students being teachers, learners, and knowers. We also get to wear these same hats.

Other students would have a personal passion for a topic, like improvisation, and would share knowledge they gained from taking outside workshops. I wouldn't stifle their sharing because the knowledge wasn't coming from me. Instead, I'd encourage them to share more. *Teacher, learner, knower.*

As I stated before, this isn't just for the classroom or other institutions of higher learning. There've been a plethora of conversations at dinner parties, birthday gatherings, weddings, coffee shops, and anywhere else that humanity gathers, where the hats of teacher, learner, and knower are passed around continuously. Oftentimes, we only come from the knower perspective, the "My way is the right way" mentality. We are listening only for the pause, so we can get our opinion out there, and not actively hear someone else's lived experience(s). This is one way we are not honoring each other's humanity.

When have you held too firmly onto your knower hat? How does it make you feel? What is your moral compass made of that just says NO, I will not allow this? When is "my way, right way" merely coming from another place; fear of the unknown, fear of being wrong, fear at all? Please take a moment and write out your answers to these questions.

When someone feels that the Work I am doing doesn't matter and that all I am trying to do is change other people, they ask, "Why would you want to spend your life doing that?"

I take a deep breath, look them in the eye to truly see their humanity, and then I speak my truth. I'm not here to change anyone. I am here to share my authentic self with the world around me and invite others to do the same, whether they listen or not. I choose to listen to other people's stories, modeling for them the respect I ask for when I am telling my story. This, to me, is freedom, being human, and having my humanity recognized, seen, and heard. Humanity validated. If we don't ask for this, if we don't share this, then we are allowing ourselves to be oppressed. We are saying that we will not learn, grow, expand, and become our biggest, fullest, and brightest.

Our brains are always learning!

Are you aware of that? If we allow ourselves to embrace our curiosity and connection about and with each other, we will continue to always be learning. This allows a simple act of meeting someone new to become learning.

Our brains are programmed to react. That is how the fight, flight, freeze, fawn mechanism works; the brain becomes aware of things that it perceives as unsafe, and reacts automatically. If we aren't actively learning, we are ruled by reactions and not by our own free will. If we take a moment to view our experiences as learning moments, then we can react based on how we want to and as influenced by our instincts. It gives this chapter even more weight from the perspective of how much of my thinking is my thinking?

And, how much of another person's humanity am I willing to not see?

Time and time again, cisgender, heterosexual, white-bodied males have consistently chosen not to see my humanity. In turn, I created just one story about this "type" of person. The fight, flight, freeze, fawn mechanism would seemingly slam itself into overdrive when someone of this characterization would enter my world.

I was at my gym when a man who fit the bill walked up to the machine next to the one I was working out on and asked me if anyone was using it. I told him no, and focused again on my own workout, fighting the single scenario in my head that was telling me to go somewhere else in the gym. I wanted to learn about how I had come to adopt such a strict idea that I was lesser than this man in front of me, and how I was allowing myself to continually uphold that idea. There was plenty of history telling me that my fear was justified, my mistrust was justified, and I knew that such a sweeping generalization had been done to me. I didn't want to live my life controlled by my reactions. I wanted my instincts, and my desire to see the humanity in everyone, to lead. I started a conversation with him, and in this situation, it became a friendship that I still have. It also became a pivotal moment of learning for myself. I have internalized the divide and conquer of white cisgendered supremacy culture, and I won't be led by my reactions.

Trusting our own personal lived experiences so that our individual personal instincts are allowed to drive us towards our authentic selves–this can only be done once we can acknowledge how much of your thinking is your thinking. If you cannot trust your thoughts/feelings/ideas to be your own, untainted by white cisgendered supremacy culture, then you cannot be your authentic self.

If we are fed ideas and beliefs of self and humanity by only one source, we will be led by reactions. If we are to truly be a lifelong learner, then we must widen our acknowledgement that the world around us is filled with many stories–all deserving to be shared, heard, and learned from. Even if what we learn is that maybe we don't want to live that way, practice that religion, or eat that food, we can allow ourselves to learn by experiencing someone else's story. This means learning from those who we don't agree with by actively listening to their stories, seeing their humanity, experiencing empathy toward their situation, and allowing them to BE. Remember, HUMANITY means recognizing ALL aspects of another, not just what we deem the pretty parts. It encompasses the ugly parts as well. We can learn from it all, leaving nothing out. I can learn from my Shadow side, as well as the side that brings light and joy into the world.

We can all be teachers and learners by gathering knowledge from all aspects of the world around us. I do not uphold white cisgendered supremacy culture. Despite its denial of my humanity, worth, and dignity, I have turned those lessons into powerful, personal medicine, focused on bringing my authentic self fully into this world.

No, it hasn't been easy.

If I wasn't a lifelong learner, I would succumb to white cisgendered supremacy culture. I've done just that in the past by trying to make people feel comfortable around me, instead of acknowledging my own need for comfort. It has manifested itself through being complacent with my own self sabotage and disassociation through drinking and drug use. I've even used being in a theater show as a way to disassociate from my desire to fit in. I would embrace the character(s) I was portraying, thinking this is how I would be seen, yet in all these instances, I wasn't learning at that moment. Being a lifelong learner is to recognize these moments, then remember that the brain is constantly growing and does not stop. The brain needs to be fed, not just the tummy. By allowing my brain to be open to growth, I can take in new experiences and learn from them.

Complacency is the danger of not having a growth mindset. This means that if I am not actively learning about myself and the world around me, I become complacent to toxic ideas, like white cisgendered supremacy culture. White cisgendered supremacy culture wants us all to fight for our right to comfort, which lulls us into complacency.

Let's think about this from the perspective of self-care. Self-care isn't just a bubble bath and a face mask. Self-care means I understand the emotions that come up for me at any given point throughout the day, and I desire that knowledge. I know the origins of those emotions and desire to learn about them through my lived experiences. If I am complacent, I don't look at the learning, I just do the action and say, "There, I feel much better!"

If we are being within integrity to ourselves as human beings who desire learning, we will search within our experiences to find the learning. The learning that is helping me to become my biggest, fullest, and brightest. Be aware of ego, because ego will come along saying that you have reached the pinnacle of learning, you are ENLIGHTENED. Once you are ripe, you are rotten. There is always more to learn.

I've watched students of mine stop learning more about the character they are portraying just because they have memorized the monologue or scene. I would ask them questions about the character, like how they feel in this situation or that, and then students would begin to understand that their journey toward that character's development is ongoing. They'd think, "I got this down" (ripe), but upon deeper reflection realize there was more to learn about this character. If the students chose not to reflect, they and the character would stay at that one point of development (rotten).

White cisgendered supremacy culture wants us all to believe that there can be just one person, one group, one idea on the top of the fictitious "Mountain of Success." A lifelong learner directly opposes this mountain, because they know that success is defined by one's lived experiences. It's the ever-transforming person who continually reaps the benefits of this life.

Just like our bellies need to be fed to nourish this complex organism called a human body, we must also feed our brains to make sure we are processing new information in a way that helps move humans forward. It is important to want to inspire one another to truly be lifelong learners. I don't want people to ever feel they have reached the pinnacle of their existence. Reaching that pinnacle is code for "right to comfort." White cisgendered supremacy culture upholds the privilege that leverages the top of the food chain mentality–a mentality which fosters a sense of complacency. See how we have now thought ourselves right back to that idea of being complete, of being done, of "Look! My Work is done." It's this vicious catch-22 that does not support the growth of humanity.

I want people to continually build a sense of belonging wherever they go. This belonging helps everyone to fully engage with life, thrive, and guide others to do the same. If people are constantly using energy figuring out how to "fit into" any given situation, they don't have time to learn. They are just busy surviving. If we feel that we belong, we bring all aspects of ourselves to any given situation. We can allow ourselves to recognize the learning to be done in those spaces.

Belonging is a key element to being lifelong learners. Many Black athletes have appeared to reach the pinnacle of their game. Being at the top of the "Mountain of Success," hasn't stopped them from being harassed by police, (e.g., Desmond Marrow[11]), when not recognized for their athletic achievements. It hasn't allowed them to be let off easy. For example, Michael Vick's[12] sentencing was so much harsher for dog fighting (going to prison for years) than Brock Turner's[13] sentencing for sexual assault (three months in jail), yet the general public think Michael Vick was let off easy and the push back on Brock's sentencing died out quickly. It hasn't stopped the entire gymnastics organization from prohibiting Simone Biles from performing particular moves. Why? Because no one else can do them. All it might take is more training and learning for others to achieve those moves. Or why not just let her be the Greatest of All Time? Why not allow her some room to shine and be the talented individual that she is? Why try to place her within the box of the status quo? White cisgendered supremacy culture is a false narrative of human achievement. It is there for itself and the upholding of a construct that "whiteness" is the dominant culture, globally. Belonging has to be present for the lifelong learner to thrive.

Have you ever felt unconditional belonging? Please share when, where, and what made it feel like unconditional belonging. If not, what would need to be different for you to feel that sense of unconditional belonging?

I am still looking for unconditional belonging that goes beyond two person interactions, and I am hopeful. I love learning. I love the amount of *new* that is present in everyday life, if we choose to see it and allow it to be a part of our lives. I love actively listening to others, and not just people, but the world around me, as well. I love asking questions such as: How is it all falling into place? Does it all fit? What does that even mean? I am so grateful for this curiosity of life that keeps me wanting more! MORE LIFE, PLEASE! I am deeply curious about the potential of the individual and how it lends itself to the potential of humanity. Keep moving forward. Always learning.

How many times a day do we ask a question to capitalize on someone else having already done the Work; to save ourselves time? Instead, could we just breathe deeply, think deeper, listen more actively, or a combination of all the above and/or more? Do *your* Work and speak *your* truth.

Invitation: Friendly reminder to hydrate.

Speaking our truth helps us to create a space where shame and fear do not rule the space. When speaking our truth, shame and fear are allowed to be looked at and unpacked with everyone involved; this helps us to discover our humanness. Being a lifelong learner is about sharing your story, knowledge, insight, and wisdom with others. Introverts, I'm not asking you to stand in a crowd of people and shout your truth at them. Yet, I do believe we all need to share on some level, whatever that is for you. Life starts on the other side of comfort. With that, again, comes a direct need for self-reflection and a strong desire to want to learn (growth mindset). It is important when we find ourselves wearing the educator hat, that we recognize what we are modeling for our listeners and what it is we expect *from* them and each other. If we cannot model that behavior *for* them, well, then maybe we need to rethink our actions in certain situations.

To be able to speak our truth, we must also learn to listen with that same authentic self. We must recognize when we are no longer listening to understand someone else, but listening instead to react and be right. Through a greater sense of community, we can dig deeper into such ideas as, "How much of your thinking is your thinking?" and "What 'masks' are worn when folx are trying to fit in? What *masks* do you see being worn in your world? What *masks* might *you* wear?" Having a community that can actively listen to us answer these questions, a community we trust and can grow in, helps us all craft a better world.

When I look at the lifelong learner and growth mindset next to white cisgendered supremacy culture, I see conflict. White cisgendered supremacy culture does not want those things and does not want them to even be a part of the conversation. If we assimilate to the status quo, we are giving in to the ideas that we are only here to work a job, have a family, and fall in line with where society wants you to go. The best way to dismantle this humanity dampening structure is to learn.

As lifelong learners, we get to nourish our creativity. We do this by inviting each person's own story, their individuality, and cultivating their choices to ignite their creativity. We get to guide and be guided along this journey, a journey that helps us to find our own light, so that through our own authentic selves we might live our lives as our biggest, fullest, and brightest selves. We cannot just jump to this quality, state, or condition of being human. It's not conducive to the growth of humanity to merely fit in, conform to societal standards, or conform to a standard that is anything but our own truth.

We can overcome the limitations of white cisgendered supremacy culture when we change our perspective, and to be able to change that perspective happens when we have somewhere we belong. The cultivation of perspective must take place by having us all not only sit together at the table of community, but we must also build, add chairs to, and polish the table together. We must also eat from the same meal being served and not keep others who have joined us at the table from eating anything at all.

The concept of teacher, learner, and knower intersects with the pivotal sentences from Chapter Two— "The past is our education. The future is our inspiration. The present moment is our creation."[14] How do we look to our past for guidance? How do we then link that to our future inspirations? What are we currently building? If we allow the status quo to dictate our very existence, we will continue to sell ourselves, and humanity, short on what we can become, and we will never comprehend that being a lifelong learner is what humanity desires on a cellular and spiritual level.

Allowing my human spirit to thrive, I ask myself these questions daily: 'How am I honoring my ancestors, each and every day? How am I living my truth? How much of my thinking is my thinking?' I am being developed by the truth of this lifetime. A lifetime in which I am doing my best to let the chains of oppressive natures, ideas, systems, slough off of my being and allow my authentic self to grow. I am allowing myself to be worthy, each and every day. I am actively balancing my mind, body, and spirit and modeling for others that self-care comes in many different forms. SOUL care is the conscious call to action of balancing the mind, body, and spirit. The seeds I am planting today are made of self-worth. I am worthy to be my authentic self. I am worthy to BE. May we all allow ourselves to be authentic to who we are, and love that person deeply.

Because we know when white people get nervous, people lose their jobs.
When white people get nervous, people get hung from trees. When white
people get nervous, babies get put in cages.
–Resmaa Menakem[15]

WHITE comfort trumps my liberation
I don't even see these situations
they flood my sensations
When the WHITE comfort trumps my liberation

"When WHITE people get nervous
People lose their jobs."

I run through my dreams wondering what it is
What it is that I am striving to be
you see, it is caught behind what you keep telling me
you keep telling me that I am not to be
Only to assimilate my creation at the expense of my liberation
WHITE comfort trumps my liberation
I don't even see these situations
they flood my sensations
When WHITE comfort trumps my liberation

"When WHITE people get nervous
Babies get put into cages."

I am trying to live a life
That makes me feel
Feel what it is to be real
Real to the world that tells me truth
WHITE comfort trumps my liberation
I don't even see these situations
They flood my sensations
When WHITE comfort trumps my liberation

"When WHITE people get nervous
People get hung from trees."

Throughout my life, I've met new people at every turn. People who would have a lasting impact on how I viewed myself, the world around me, and myself within that world. I began to make connections with my past, my history, my story. I began to see the interconnectedness of my life—how it was all influencing the other, bringing forward, each day, my purpose: being an educator.

Then the roadblocks, as I used to call them, started speaking up in my subconscious and conscious mind. They'd say things like, "Who are you to think you deserve comfort?" "You are stupid." "You are unworthy of life itself." These thoughts led me to do my own personal Work. I found language that helped me find the name for these roadblocks—Shadow.

The Shadow is the part of oneself created by believing what other people, society, pop culture, and gaslighting have negatively taught you to believe about yourself. The Shadow doesn't serve you, until you finally learn to recognize it as a tool to help you see your truth. A truth that helps guide you toward learning, being a lifelong learner. Those lies are someone else's Work, not your own.

In Chapter One, I shared about the physical abuse from my father, psychological abuse from my father and society, fighting to belong. Fighting to be loved, fighting. Each of these situations were traumatic during a time when my cognitive brain, and my human spirit, couldn't comprehend everything that these situations were creating inside me. Each of these situations either created Shadow or fed an already existing one. The intimacy of a father, the betrayal of a dear friend, the box that society wants us to fit into are all fuel for the fires that burn a person's self-worth so badly that it becomes Shadow.

Invitation: Take a moment, set down the book, and roll your shoulders backward a few times. Now roll them forward. Breathe in and pull your shoulders toward your ears. Now breathe out slowly and release. Do this three times.

My mom, Glenda Lou Sorrels, was born and raised in Central Illinois. Her Irish, German, and Swedish blood passed along to me and my siblings. My parents met roughly a decade before the *Loving v. Virginia* Supreme Court decision[16] was passed. My mom knew what it meant to be seen as "other," especially to the family that kicked her out for loving a Black man. Whenever there was trouble at school, it was my mom who came in to deal with it. When my father was abusive to me, there was my mom with a tight-lipped, disapproving look on her face that she'd turn away, so as not to bring the wrath of my father upon her. At first, I thought she didn't care, then I realized that she could comfort me more easily after the fact if he thought she was on his side of the scolding I was getting. Small phrases of loving support she'd whisper to me as she held me when I cried, "Oh, you are going to be alright. Remember you are Mama's strong baby boy. You are Mama's beautiful baby boy." And as I got older, it became, "Your father had a rough life before all of us. He doesn't always know how to deal with that fact. Remember to not take on his burdens, those are for him to carry, not you. Remember, as you get older, how you want to be treated and how you want to treat others." I see now how these phrases helped me to better understand the Work that it takes to uproot the Shadow, look at it, learn from it, and not let it rule my life. At the same time as I was getting these tools from my mom, Shadow was being created within me.

I went to a summer Christian camp when I was eight years old. That is when I first felt my attraction to the same gender awakening within me. It wasn't sexual, it was soul stirring. I had this counselor, and I couldn't get enough of looking at him, being around him, and just hearing him speak. He was eighteen years old, and I followed him everywhere. It was confusing when I left camp that summer and cried the entire way home. I kept saying it was because I was going to miss camp, but it was him that I was already missing.

I began to ask my older sister how she knew that she liked the boy she was dating, why they were going to movies, as well as other relationship advice. I was fascinated that they went on dates, which was something my parents did not do. Then, I began asking questions to my Sunday school teacher. When I asked if boys could be with boys, I got the "It's a sin" speech. I never asked anyone about it again. Then, new neighbors moved in across the street. I saw "him" and all those same feelings from summer camp came back. Mixed with the "It's a sin" brainwashing, Shadow and feelings of unworthiness were strengthened.

"Truth, Dare … Double Dare."

Did he pause for a moment before he said it?!? "Double Dare?"

I was ten years old and he was twelve. It was the middle of summer in Minnesota. We were sleeping out in the camper. Other times when we played Truth, Dare, Double Dare, it was with other lakeshore kids, who only lived there during the summer. A double dare meant some kind of human-to-human contact. Touching naked butts together, kissing someone, kissing someone's naked butt. I knew it was a courageous, manly thing to do, to say …

"Double Dare," came shooting out of my mouth, released from the restraints of the unknown.

Here was the only kid, besides some at school, that didn't call me names like nigger, fag, sissy boy, tar baby, Black faggot. And because of that, and my ever growing attraction to other boys, I had a crush on him. I always wanted to be next to him, with him. Riding bikes, swimming, building forts, hanging out in the forts, Matchbox car racing … sleeping out in the camper.

"Double Dare you …"

There it was, the gauntlet had been thrown, the tighty-whities removed, permission to release my resistance to physical contact with him. Alas, I was ten.

… "YUCK! THAT'S GROSS!" came out of my mouth, yet inside, I couldn't resist that strong urge to want to be closer to him, close to the point of contact!!

"You picked it, you gotta do it!"

I slowly sat up on my side of the camper, looked across at his summer tan skin and tighty-whities, laying there in the moonlight. Every part of me wanted that intimacy, that connection, to show him that I was a good friend, trustworthy and loyal. This was the start of him and I finding any opportunity that we could to be naked with each other and, eventually, for me to "service" him.

Then it stopped. … Four years later. It all stopped.

The gravel underneath my feet creates small clouds of dust behind me as I walk down the dirt road toward the lake. I stare out over the lake and proceed to take off my shoes and socks. I wade out into the water, up to my knees, my crotch, my stomach, my chest. I feel my body slip under the water when it reaches my shoulders. My world has turned into a liquid bliss. No weight pushing down on my feet. No dust clouds blowing away in the wind. Just the sound of my body functioning in its everyday manner.
No air.
Come up out of the water? Shadow says, No.
No air.
Panic in my body. Heart beating faster. Pounding. Expel all my air. Sink to the bottom. Laying there on this underwater grave. Fully embracing all that Shadow has to offer.
I can't do this. Shadow whispers, "Yes, you can." Tension around my eyes begins to relax as my heart slows.
What if he were to come down here while I was underwater? What then? WHAT THEN? **WHAT THEN?**
Breaking through the surface of the water, spraying the air around me with

small water droplets as I suck in as much air as I can.
Panic subsiding.
Getting my bearings.
Look to shore.
Grass.
Trees.
Shoes.
Socks.
Water runs out of my kinky hair, down into my eyes. Sting. The tears finally release.
Standing in the shoulder deep water, adding my salty tears to its depths.

There are times when it has been hard to resist my Shadow whispering in my ear that "I wasn't good enough," that "I was all the names people called me," AND that "I was the things they said I was behind my back." I see now that the world is filled with many hes, those who just weren't there. I see now how Shadow needed these moments to grow, live, and to influence my life. During Shadow's growth, it was so easy to think about and attempt to take my life. This was what Shadow expected of me.

Invitation: Please take a moment and take a sip of water.

Shadow feeds on reaction. It wants you to be reactive. If you are reactive, there is no learning, no growing. Shadow is the antithesis of being fully realized from a place of authenticity and dignity. Looking at Shadow makes me uncomfortable. White cisgendered supremacy culture feeds the right to comfort so you will never uncover or look at your Shadows, because it is so hard. It is easier to not look at those things.

My Shadow has also hurt other people. It has kept me from feeling worthy of having close intimate relationships — romantic or not. I always felt that I needed to continue to make everyone else happy or joyful. When a dark mood came over me, I wouldn't share that with anyone. I was not sharing all of myself with the people around me. I was too busy trying to fit in. It was not until I started working through this in therapy that I realized how much I had hurt other people by not sharing all aspects of myself with them. It was a form of gaslighting. I was lying to them by not being my authentic self. I would change things about myself as a way to manipulate the way they felt about me. All this was grown out of my own Shadow.

In the past, I would try to run away from Shadow. This left me feeling unworthy and alone. By owning my Shadow, I was able to offer myself forgiveness. Then, I was able to see how my Shadow hurt other folks, apologize to them, and hopefully receive forgiveness from them. This is all me standing in my authenticity, by holding myself accountable for my Shadow. This is something that I didn't learn from our government and leaders.

Confronting my trauma head-on with my truth. Trauma reinforces my Shadow's way of seeing myself. Only through working with a professional have I been guided to see how these traumas shaped my perception of myself. I've gone through therapy and looked at my own Shadows, dissecting them and changing some of those old beliefs. Our government has also caused these traumas on this stolen land and in other countries, but will not look at its own trauma to heal.

Genocide, slavery, amassing wealth under the guise of a free market, hunger, houselessness, addiction, corporations over humanity, and a myriad of other traumatic catalysts happening in the United States, run throughout its past, present, and perceivable (yet changeable) future. These traumas are not only within US citizens, but are also found methodically intertwined throughout the current bureaucratic systems and the systems that built the United States.

This is the foundation of white cisgendered supremacy culture. The United States is so afraid of the trauma inflicted upon the people it has oppressed and marginalized that it will not allow the truth to be taught within its own education system. How much more powerful we could be as a nation if we uplifted humanity through the healing of these traumas? Ownership of the responsibility of this healing is paramount to the growth of our nation.

Some of my Shadow was created out of what was passed down from my father, caused by generational trauma from being transported to and enslaved on this continent. A disconnection took place during the transportation of my ancestors from the west coast of Continental Africa to the east coast of the United States. I don't have insight into the joy and history of my lineage because it was stripped from my ancestors. There is missing history living in me, creating a void.

My eighth-grade-educated father did not have the tools to deal with these things. He was the second generation out of slavery. He was in the thick of the battle over his body, feeling that he was lesser than, that he was supposed to be enslaved, that he was supposed to do the work for the white people. Even though he was the second generation out of slavery, he was still enslaved. When you are enslaved you are enslaved in mind, body and spirit: Body — in shackles, Mind — through gaslighting, Spirit — there was no way out.

Colonization is the Shadow of the nation, the country, and the world. It is the Shadow that a majority of people will not look at. If they do, then they can't colonize you. They cannot take your home away from you or use your resources. They would have to see you for your humanity. We keep feeding that Shadow, the one that is limiting humanity. Colonization, white-bodied supremacy, and so forth, hold up the hierarchy that promises people can pull themselves up by their bootstraps. That, one day, they can reach the top and be "in charge." That is just an illusion.

Those in power have continued to amass wealth, land, and monies while the rest of us have just amassed trauma, not to say that those in power do not have their own trauma.

When will we recognize the gross disservice these traumas do to everyone? When will we recognize that we all need to heal? When will we begin to heal?

Shadow does not go away. It will always be a part of me, but now it is a source of empowerment. Now, I see more clearly when I am selling myself short. I see more clearly when it is not my authentic self presenting forward. I see more clearly how I am not upholding humanity with certain words or actions. I know now to embrace the darkness and to not fear it. Shadow has much to teach us all.

What are your Shadows that you have from your own personal history? What are some of your Shadows that have come from a generational/collective history? What Work are you doing to heal from those?

*If anything in this chapter has brought up deeply rooted blockages (quick to anger, confusion, feeling that chaos is all around, continual negative self-talk, etc.) to your authenticity, please seek professional help. #lovemytherapist

worthy & belonging

I stare out into the faces of you. … Blink.
Focus on yet another. … Blink.
Focus on an empty chair. … Blink.

Eyes seek warmth like that of infrared vision
But not only in the darkness of night, but in the darkness of my
days
Always seeking out that warmth
That warmth … that … that warmth

Can't you tell me where it is?

Feel with me
Touching with an inner energy that is not visible to the sheltered
eye
Feel with me

Scanning deeper into the faces of you. … Blink.
Unfocused. Not knowing. Not knowing what is to come next
Only growing in my search for THAT warmth
Down that road, that path, that sidewalk, that lighted tunnel

The lights. They give off warmth
A knowing of growing
Growing for myself
Looking to share that growth with

The lights' warmth is comforting
Only for a while though

Then, back down that street. … Blink.
A small sound. … Blink.
Another.

Hold my eyes closed
Cool tones coming at me
Don't search
They say
Don't search
Just let it flow out until another connects
Just-------let---------it-------floooooooowwwwwww … open my eyes
I stare out into the faces of you

*Fitting in is about assessing a situation and becoming who you need to be
to be accepted. Belonging, on the other hand, doesn't require us to change
who we are; it requires us to be who we are.*
–Brené Brown, *The Gifts of Imperfection*[17]

Mrs. Canfield, from the fourth grade, is my earliest recollection of a person, other than my mother, who radiated kindness and unconditional love toward me. This was done by not requiring me to change who I was. To be in her classroom was to be Me. When I look at the quote above, I'm reminded that Mrs. Canfield not only radiated a sense of belonging, but of unconditional belonging.

For instance, I had gotten into yet another fight with a fellow student because of a racial slur. Mrs. Canfield sat us both down and explained the bias of that racial slur by talking about the hurtful ignorance of the slur and how it just wasn't the truth. She commented on how beautiful, intelligent, kind, and loving I and all the other students were. She continued to say that she knew that the student who used the racial slur didn't understand its meaning. Then she asked the student, "Now that you know the meaning, will you use it again?"

"No," the student replied and never used it again (at least not against me). This was fourth grade, and I remember so clearly how she went into detail about where the racial slur came from. I had never heard its definition or its hateful history. I was in awe of her intelligence and her willingness to share, and that she did this in a way that didn't cause me, or the other student, any more harm. Lovingly and magically building belonging.

She showed me that I wanted everybody I came into contact with to feel that same sense of being seen, being heard—unconditional belonging from me. I guess I have desired a sense of belonging all my life. Now, I can wander through my lived experiences and, though I may not remember everyone's name, I can share something about our time together that impacted my life. I have been told countless times that I have positively impacted someone's life. All of my life, I have been a conduit for truth and guidance, which leads to clarity and support for others.

Sifting through my skills, my talents, and how I have used them throughout my life; I began to embrace the truth that I enjoy bringing people together and allowing them to share their own skills and talents. Then, we collaborate to build. To build belonging. Building something that has been longed for, but never seen, at least not in this creation. It has many voices and many faces at the table. Shifting, lifting, growing into being. This is the magic of feeling worthy and belonging.

Fitting in is like gaslighting yourself. You begin to think that this way of being in the world is your truth, when it couldn't be any further from your truth. Fitting in does nothing to help guide a person to their authentic self. Fitting in inhibits the growth of humanity. Reflecting on all of this helped me define belonging for myself, my classroom culture, and now for the world I am crafting. Not only belonging, but unconditional belonging.

"Matthew, I have had other teachers come to me and say that you made the meeting all about you," the principal said to me.

This comment came after a staff meeting where I emotionally shared something a student told me. The student told me that they did not feel supported by the teachers in the hallway who clearly heard that student being called a homophobic slur. The comment by the principal became the first of many that crippled my authenticity and further fed my Shadow, which in turn started me down the road of just fitting in, and never feeling a sense of belonging.

After that comment, and others like it, I stopped sharing my opinions in staff meetings. I would make myself small in those meetings. And I didn't venture out into the school campus much either. I couldn't acknowledge the exclusionary language I heard in the hallways, the confederate flag patches on hats and jackets, or the energy of judgment that I felt in most hallways about who and what they thought me to be. Fitting in equaled survival. It took a ton of energy and a toll on my soul. If this is how I was feeling, how were my students being affected by this culture? This is definitely not what I wanted the school culture to be, and I definitely did not want it in my classroom. I wanted my students and myself to be liberated from others' ideas of who we should be. As we read in the Brené Brown quote, belonging "requires us to be who we are."

When I was going through my teenage years, I worked really hard just to fit in because that seemed like the only way to survive.

- Participate in every kind of activity you can–that way people wouldn't say that you were lazy.
- Study hard–that way people wouldn't call you stupid.
- Make 'em laugh–that way they wouldn't see how lonely, afraid, and depressed you were.

My truth was never allowed to be in the room. It could live in my thoughts, journals, and conversations I had out loud with myself as I walked in the woods, but those were the only places. The rest of the time, when I allowed my authentic self to BE in the world, I was bullied, I fought, and I definitely didn't feel like I belonged.

These lived experiences influenced my determination to find somewhere to belong. To walk in the world filled with all the unconditional love, time, effort, support, encouragement, self-worth, patience, understanding, accountability, and authenticity, I gave to my students and everyone else around me … for myself. Believing in me with that same passion and determination, guilt-free, and full of knowing. Not only did I need to want this for myself and my students, but modeling it for them was paramount to living my worth, and building unconditional belonging.

It is still difficult for me to fully live it, daily. Shadow, and our long history, has a way of sneaking in and telling me that I'm not worthy of any of this. I don't want others to have this difficult time with something that should be as simple as believing in oneself.

Invitation: Please take some time to get up and go for a walk.

After retiring from the classroom, I opened myself up to what to do next. I spoke, taught, listened, and created the process of *Crafting Your Equity Lens*.[18] Through workshops with me, participants can go through the process of unpacking how much of their thinking is their own thinking in order for them to create their own Equity Lens that will drive their choices and decisions from a place of authenticity. My definition of an Equity Lens: something crafted by the individual, utilizing their own lived experiences. It must be ever-evolving as one meets new people, has new experiences, gains knowledge and wisdom, and recognizes what their definition of anti-racist work is. It must be something that grows into being *your Truth Vision*. It has integrity, accountability, vulnerability, self-worth, and unconditional love at its core. It is building unconditional belonging. It is a call to action.

I feel deeply in my heart of hearts that this is the Work I am to bring into the world, to help humanity expand itself into its biggest, fullest, and brightest. To this day, I have trouble believing that I am worthy of this offering. How can I be worthy when, on some days, I see myself as society does? Lazy, hurtful, and harmful to self and others, stupid, filled with anxiety, worthless. When these voices want to be in the forefront of my thoughts, I look to my past, as *our past is our education*. I look at all the times these voices lied to me, and I see clearly that what the voices are saying has been used to keep my authentic self from living courageously, bravely, and freely. My truth: I am courageous. I am brave. I am free. I am worthy.

All of these voices seem quieter when I am actually building unconditional belonging. It's almost as if Shadow knows that I will never belong in a society so thoroughly enmeshed with white cisgendered supremacy culture. There is a glitch in its system; when we build towards unconditional belonging. Just enough of a glitch for me to help others liberate themselves and do their Work, and for all of us to begin to build the NEW that is filled with truth, integrity, belonging, and love.

One of the loudest voices in my head says that wealth equates evil. Capitalism has been proven time and time again, in my sphere of influence, to cause harm to humanity. It doesn't allow folx to truly be fully realized, because so much of their time and effort is spent on making money to survive. What I mean by "survive" is one must have a source of income to have their most basic needs met. This includes clean water, food, shelter, clothes, and basic healthcare. I was born poor, raised poor, lived as a starving artist, and even when I became an educator, I funded my programs while I taught. Now here I am. Rich in friends, experiences, empathy, love, and much more. My pocket book is still, by others' standards, poor.

These basic needs are then tied back into the dominant culture's ideas of success. Being able to survive is success for most. There are plenty of the basic needs available for humanity to survive, so why are there people starving? Dying from exposure to the elements or lack of clean water? The dominant culture believes amassing wealth and material goods shows status and worth. To get that to happen, everyone must believe that to be true. What about the wealth of a society that believes in itself? What about the abundance of growth that humanity is capable of if we allow ourselves to be fully realized? It is staggering the amount of energy a person gives out in a lifetime just to make enough money to have food to eat.

These mindsets are all based on half-truths and blatant lies about what has worth:

"You aren't worthy of love if you don't use our shampoo."

"You aren't worthy of good health if you don't have a *good* job and career."

"You aren't worthy of a good job and career unless you go to college."

"You aren't worthy of college unless you graduate from a *good* high school."

It is a vicious cycle that does not support the expansion of humanity to its biggest, fullest, and brightest. And it all plays off of our personal sense of self-worth. No wonder I struggle so much just to believe in myself.

How about you? Do you believe in yourself? Do you feel worthy of the world you dream about? Please take a moment to write about your answers to these questions.

When I am focused on my Work, it is easy for me to see that I am worthy of being paid for my offerings to humanity. I have worked hard to hone the skills necessary to bring liberation from the indoctrination of a society built on gaslighting people into believing they are worthless until they can monetarily afford to be otherwise. Liberate your mind, body, and human spirit from these dehumanizing beliefs and ideas. I am allowing myself to accept the payment of my worth, as well as guiding others to liberate themselves and also know this truth.

My growth is centered around the truth of this lifetime, in which I am doing my best to let the chains of oppressive natures, ideas, and systems slough off of my being and allow my authentic self to grow. For instance, I am allowing myself to be worthy today and get a massage. This massage will help me to balance my mind, body, and spirit. It will also let me model for others that soul care comes in many different forms. The seeds I am planting today are made of self-worth. I am worthy to be my authentic self. I am worthy to BE. May we all allow ourselves to be authentic to who we are and love that person deeply, because we are worthy.

Take a moment. Make a list of ways you can practice soul care, showing yourself that you are WORTH that love. Circle one that you could do today.

When making the decision to move to Hawai'i, I allowed myself to accept the offer of my dear friends, Eric and Christopher. Allowing myself the grace that I am worthy of living next to my dear friends in such a healing place. I AM WORTHY!! Believing in myself sits at the intersection of mind, body, spirit, calling forth the balance of the three. Every day of my life is that moment, the moment that I can be who I truly am, and that is enough.

By utilizing my Equity Lens, I stay present in these moments of truth and unconditional belonging. The personal Equity Lens is needed to help ourselves see when the dominant culture impresses ideas upon us that do not align with our authentic self. I embrace my authenticity at this moment. I have realized that one of the greatest gifts that my Equity Lens is giving me is this insight into me. The authentic ME. The person who was bombarded by societal norms, dominant culture, status quo, family, friends, education, church, and lovers. Ideas of who I should be are being challenged daily.

Through this challenge of asking myself daily, throughout the day, "How much of your thinking is your thinking?" I am seeing what isn't mine and what is. Living my Equity Lens every day has allowed my vision of myself to be clear. THIS is belonging at its base. I am beginning to belong to myself.

How can I step into, or even hold space for, a room based on unconditional belonging if I don't belong to myself?

When my authenticity is so clouded by the world around me, it never truly feels like I belong. Now that my true self is stepping more and more into being, I AM finding belonging even in spaces where I thought I didn't belong. I am worthy to belong anywhere that I find myself. This doesn't come from a place of self-aggrandizement or ego, it comes from a place of recognition. Recognizing that I am part of this planet. I am not above it, I AM it. I am stardust turned into blood and bone.

Balancing mind, body, and spirit has helped me see, feel, hear, taste, and smell the truth of these last couple of sentences. When will we allow ourselves to know what we have always been? That we are OF this planet, not above it. That we are human beings, mammals, stardust. We are deserving of our humanity. We deserve to thrive, expand, and become part of, for we never truly left. We have just thought ourselves out of our place within this world. Authenticity is directly linked to worthiness, belonging, and allowing ourselves to BE. When I have those moments of feeling ungrounded and not part of, I stand in the grass, sand, soil—earth connection, called "grounding"—allowing myself to be with the greater world, instead of above it or disconnected from it. I believe in me. I believe in me. I believe in me. I believe in me. I BELIEVE IN ME.

Do you believe in you? What realizations might you be having about yourself while reading this chapter? This book? When was the last time you placed your skin onto the earth? Feeling its healing touch, allowing yourself to be healed, feeling a part of, and not above.

Invitation: Please say this aloud, and add your own affirmations, as well:

I am worthy of believing in myself. I am worthy of love. I am worthy of respect. I am worthy of my humanity. I am worthy of your friendship. I am worthy of abundance. I am worthy of learning. I am worthy of being seen. I am worthy of being heard. I am worthy. (Bonus–Do this while standing barefoot on the earth.)

Belonging to myself. Empowered to be my truth in this existence. Unconditional Belonging—Unconditional Love—Unconditional Existence. Allowing myself to just BE. WHAT THE WHAT?!?!? SHOOK TO THE CORE! These concepts began the unraveling of what has been placed upon me by others, feelings that aren't mine. I am me. I love, therefore I am.

Unconditional love comes from the innermost part of my heart. I'm doing my best to remind, encourage, and show people that they *are* love and they are loved. I am doing my best to model this every day, all day. I am building this through helping others craft their Equity Lens. I am shaping the world around me through my Equity Lens. The energy of this giving echoes through the ethers, seven generations ago and seven generations from now.

eight
dreams

My dreams started out as a place of magnificence. I'd dream of comforting temperatures; Minnesota can be blazing humid hot and frigid rigid cold. I dreamed of large fields of grass, stretching out for miles and miles. Shimmering in the sunlight, the grass would be so welcoming, caring, and loving even. I just wanted to run and run through the fields, letting the fields nourish my soul. *The different color font denotes the different dreams that I have had.*

When you look at me, what do you see?
Black
Gay
Male
Dollars

When you look at me, what do you feel?
Scared
Aroused
Angry
Powerful

When you look at me, what do you hear?
Rhythm
Pulse
Swoosh
Cha-ching

dreams

When you look at me, do you ever see my humanity?

How many times have I looked into the mirror over the years and not seen any joy, laughter, curiosity, creativity, or life looking back at me? I am not here to blame. I am here to grow. My life has been filled with being "the other." Othering has caused me to be bitter, jaded, harsh, and unable to dream.

I am walking down the street. No one is taking any real notice of me. Those who make eye contact smile and nod, some say, "Hello," and I continue on with my day. I feel no need to protect myself, my being, my very existence from stares, furrowed brows, piercing looks, or the occasional thrown racial or sexual slur. This world I am dreaming in, this world has no need for those things. Everyone is feeling, and being, belonging. Gravity doesn't seem so strong. I feel like I am grounded and at the same time light and floaty. I am in need of this in my life. I realize that I will be waking up soon. I don't dwell on that fact. Instead, I take a running leap and shoot up thirty feet into the air, hanging there for a moment, and slowly start to descend back to the earth. I notice that if I kick my legs like I'm swimming, I can slowly rise back up. If I dance in the sky, I stay at the level that I am at and if I leap, I propel myself in the direction I leapt. My smile is so big. I feel the tension in my face, knowing that lately in my waking hours it hasn't gotten much of a chance to be used. I just keep on smiling and working that muscle. I notice that folx down below are waving and smiling, and some are launching themselves into the sky. Is this what humans could evolve into? Can we all break free of the confines of gravity, for small bursts? I decide that I want to land. I stick my arms out to either side and flap down, instead of up, and down I go, pausing before impact and settling down to earth. My smile is still working my facial muscles!!! "I am loving this dream, people!" I shout this out to no one in particular, but receive several shouts back in agreement. I continue on my walk, wondering what else has changed. I feel a bit hungry, so I stop at a pretzel dog stand. The person serving up the pretzel dogs is beautifully ambiguous in their gender identity. Their smile is so full of compassion, generosity, understanding, and unconditional love. I just melt as they hand me a pretzel dog. I reach for my money and they laugh. "There is no money here. This is my craft, and I give it generously to humanity." Whoa! I nod my gratitude, afraid to use my voice because it is choked with emotion. What is my craft? What am I generously giving to humanity? What do I …

Beepbeepbeep … beepbeepbeep … I am awakened by my alarm. Dreaming is good for the soul. Nurturing my creativity. I will begin to build what I see in my dreamtime.

Sometimes, I dream that I'm walking around in different locations on this planet, in other dimensions, in other worlds. And in this dream, I am casually making eye contact with other beings and exchanging energies through that look. It is powerful and empowering. I try it in my waking moments as well. Acknowledging and allowing these energy exchanges to be lived out by saying hello, smiling, nodding, stopping and looking even deeper. Would you ever do such a thing? What would it take for you to acknowledge these moments of energetic recognition between you and what might be called a stranger? Aren't we just acknowledging the humanity within each other? Is that really such a hard thing to do?

I'm dreaming of a world where all needs are met. No hunger. No lack of clean water. No lack of shelter. I want to know what we can be if we didn't have ideas pushed into our heads of what we are supposed to be. HUMANITY, where have you gone?

I see the glow of your eyes now
It wasn't there before
I see the way in which all things around you are you
I see how we are part of this
We aren't above this, no
I see the glow in your eyes now

I'm not sure where I'm going, but it feels good to be in this space, in this way. I'm beginning to feel the words more fully within my moments. Nothing is set in stone, especially the who and what of me. I hope that you feel that you, too, are not set in stone?

The clouds are moving so quickly above my head. They are shifting in color from a pearlescent glowing white to peachy pink, from flamingo to deep reddish orange, to purple. Night has fallen. I can see easily in the dark. Not in infrared, but in auras. I can tell where something or someone is by the flow of colorful energy around their shape, or the shape of a structure, tree, shrub, or rock. I am not going anywhere in particular. I don't feel a need to be somewhere. I am just moving my body through space, feeling the dimensionality of my being, mobile. The stars were strung across the sky following the setting sun, as if someone was drawing the shade down over a window. A shade made of billions of stars twinkling. I inhale and can smell the rich loam of the earth, and it makes me feel ALIVE. As my feet roll me down the lane, I am curious about the other creatures moving through the dusk, soon to be night. Curious as to how it could be any other way than this, it feels so good and right. The smell is shifting to something sweet and flavorful. I find myself under a fruit tree. I can tell by the fruit's aura, it is a peach tree. With darkness deepening, the smell of the peaches is thrumming in the air, telling me to nourish my body. I

The waking hours are filled with manifestations of the glimpses my dreams give me. Glimpses into what humanity wants to be—its biggest, fullest, and brightest. This keeps me moving forward. This keeps me dreaming.

I dream of a time when humanity begins to understand that our lives are filled with learning. We'll know what we like, dislike, will stand or sit down for, walk away from, and most importantly, what it is that keeps us motivated in this existence. Do we really only see ourselves making money to survive? I need to pay this bill or that bill. When will we start to understand that like our bodies, our souls need feeding and nourishing too?

Recognizing that I am dreaming into reality our very own authenticity of being human. We are more than the boxes that the dominant culture's ideas of us are. We can be so much more than just the identifiers we are given or have given ourselves. From an early age we are encouraged to dream, and then it seems like we come to an age where all that dreaming is forgotten, just so that it is easier on us when we follow along and fill in the boxes with our very existence. I am dreaming myself and humanity out of those boxes.

How many of you don't dream any more, while sleep and/or awake? What was your last dream while sleeping? What have you always dreamed of being/having/doing but have just not done it? Can you remember the dreams you had in your youth? What age were you? When are dreams allowing our subconscious to actually help us to expand our very being? What is the difference between a dream and a goal?

I dream of allowing the joy my heart desires to be fully realized within this lifetime.
I dream of flying through the ether, making room in my head and heart for the newness of all that I am experiencing.
I dream of a time when all humans have all their basic needs met, and money has become a thing of the past.
I dream of not thinking on a binary track, but on an ever expanding, outward in all directions way.
I dream of being fully realized in this short existence I have, THIS time around.
I dream that I give grace to myself and others with ease and comfort.
I dream of embracing my mom again.
I dream of foods that make all my senses feel alive and active.
I dream of the children that no one gives a second thought to.
I dream that beyond the sky there are other beings who want to meet, exchange knowledge and histories, and also desire the expansion of the Universe to be filled with joyful abundance for all creatures big and small.
I dream all of this for the rest of humanity as well.

Imagine if we taught our children from a place of humanity. Empathy, compassion, integrity, respect, responsibility, and accountability; all wrapped up and presented from a place of unconditional love.

Imagine if their intrinsic motivations were actively acknowledged and nurtured, allowing that motivation to lead them to the softer skills of reading, writing, and arithmetic.

Imagine the world the youth would build by leading from their hearts. A place where being a lifelong learner wasn't a hope, but just a part of life. A world of active listeners, breathing compassion and deeper understanding into every interaction. A world that is awash with belonging.

Imagine a world where all basic human needs are met, because we teach our children from a place of HUMANITY.

My eyes slowly open. I can feel my body. I can reach out to the corners of my mind, and I am not sure if this moment is reality or another dream. I am standing in water that stops mid-thigh. The water is refreshing, but not warm. I can see that it stretches out in front of me for a long distance. My feet are in sand that feels comforting and uplifting. The surface of the water is undisturbed, as if it were a mirror, and it looks to be of the same mid-thigh depth as far as I can see. I am not wearing any clothes, and the freedom I feel from the sun on all my skin is empowering. What is behind me? I turn slowly and behind me is exactly what is in front of me. I don't feel any sort of way from this newly found information. It is just the truth of this moment, a moment in my life. Spiral. I look around, turning slowly. Spiral. I began to move off of the spot I am currently in. I am slowly expanding away from the center of that moment. Spiral. As I move further away, in concentric circles, widening in an outward space, I realize that I can sense the pathway of the … spiral. Looking toward the center, I can now see there is a hole where I started. Did I come up through the hole? Fall down from the up into that spot so that now there is a hole? I notice that my spiral has me about 200 yards from the center of the spiral, and the spiral glows a faint shade of lavender gold where I have walked. It is humming a note that makes my heart feel seen, heard, and loved. The concept of time has no place here. I am now roughly a mile away from the center. My spiral seems to be evenly spaced and circularly spot on. The depth of the glowing lavender golden hue has deepened. The water is making no sound. I was so fixated on the spiral that I had not noticed until this moment that there was no splashing. I exhale loudly. I can hear that, and the water is making no sound. Spiral. I begin to make out something on the horizon, in all directions. It is as if I am confined inside a sphere. Spiral. No sense of

dread, fear, or any emotion, I just keep walking my spiral.
The horizon is glowing a peachy salmon color, as if it is
made of seashell. All my senses are alive, tingling, moving,
stretching, being. I look to the center of the spiral. It is
miles away, yet I can count each ripple of my spiral, all the
way back to the hole in the center …

I've been expanding into my skills for public speaking, storytelling, empathy, compassion, building community, and holding space. All of this dreaming itself into building communities that are TRUE communities.

I use American psychiatrist M. Scott Peck's definition of the true meaning of community from his book *The Different Drum: Community Making and Peace.* He defines true community as "a group of individuals who have learned how to communicate honestly with each other, whose relationships go deeper than their masks of composure, and who have developed some significant commitment to 'rejoice together, mourn together,' and to 'delight in each other, make others' conditions our own.'"[19] This falls in line with everything I believe of a true community and what it should be.

He goes on to say that true communities must have the following characteristics. They must:

- Be inclusive
- Be realistic and have consensus
- Have contemplation and self-awareness
- Be a safe place
- Show vulnerability and efforts to make peace
- Be able to express differences gracefully
- Be a place where all are leaders
- Have an atmosphere of love, peace, wisdom, and power[20]

All of these characteristics speak to my heart and my belief system. I believe that we, as humanity, would do best in groups of one hundred or less. I'd call these groups pods. I'd structure these pods from M. Scott Peck's ideals and make sure that each and every pod had all the basic needs fulfilled.

Supporting humanity on its most basic level—guaranteeing food, water, and shelter—must come first! From there, I would eliminate money. Everything would be based on a barter system. It is what has been coined the *Star Trek* utopia. You see, Gene Roddenberry, *Star Trek* creator, set the series in a future where money is obsolete. Everyone has the basics, and nobody has to work for monetary sums to purchase the basic necessities.

Your skills would be nurtured and shared with your pod, benefiting everyone within that pod. We would be lovingly supported as our cognitive brains grew, and our intrinsic motivators would be nurtured knowing that those motivators would benefit everyone in the pod later in life. I believe that if I had been lovingly supported from birth, this society wouldn't be so farfetched. This is the type of society that many Indigenous peoples, who have been massacred by the dominant culture, were nurturing before. I am looking for the balance of what has been mostly eradicated, and what humanity presently offers. Not only am I worthy of this type of true community, ALL humanity is worthy of it as well.

What could I build with this life of mine if all of me was lovingly supported by the world around me? End this chapter by taking a moment to answer this question, and THANK YOU for speaking your truth.

100

no more dreams. ... action

Your words fly outta your mouth
Little tiny missiles shooting out and about
Where they land explodes into pain and frustration
Knowing that here we are again
Leading with what built this nation
Violence, trauma, and greed
Nothing about this tells me I am free
Free of the pain your words inflict
No, like tiny little insects
I just feel each and every impact
Impacting my dreams of just being me
No more dreams, I just want to BE

"But I am the good guy!" I've heard this cry of astonishment, anger, frustration, shock, and dismay from an array of people. It usually followed some comment or statement that was dehumanizing to a marginalized group, or multiple groups, and when I spoke my truth about how their comment impacted me. *The road to hell is paved with good intentions.* With the amount of lies and gaslighting that is part of Amerikkkan culture, it is no wonder that folx have a difficult time with the truth of their "good intentions," and the impact they have on the people in the room.

In my lived experiences, I've been fearful of my physical well-being, my job, being liked, as well as actually speaking my truth when it came to experiencing comments others made in the name of helping or supporting others. These aggressive comments are categorized as microaggressions, which are subtle, but offensive comments or actions that unintentionally or unconsciously reinforce a stereotype about non-dominant groups. When discussing this with folx, I remind them that at its core it is still an aggression.

I continually hear people getting hung up on the "dream" aspect of creating a just and equity-based world. One that leads with humanity and allows people's authenticity to bring us together to make a decision about the betterment of the community. It doesn't need to be the perfect new world, or one where each and every person must hold the line of activism. Conversations with family around white supremacy, standing up at a meeting in solidarity with the marginalized group, and/or making a meal that feeds those who are in constant deliberations; all of these actions dismantle white supremacy, and all positions are important. We need to move beyond the dream and into action by refusing to uphold what is already defined by white supremacy as "how it must be done." Lean into your curiosity of the truth of your personal history and the truth of the history of our nation, of humanity. *The past is our education.* Learn and grow from it, but do not get stuck in it.

Embrace the connection with your authentic self. Learning that we have all been indoctrinated into the colonizers' ideas of white supremacy, patriarchy, capitalism, and hierarchy. Growing toward our connections with each other, through our unlearning of our indoctrination, allows not only our personal transformation, but also the transformation of humanity.

Allowing ourselves to be passionate about our creativity frees us from the shackles of the dominant culture, and allows us to not just dream big, but to begin to build. When we only know white supremacy culture and we are given the opportunity to build something NEW, we sometimes get stuck with only knowing what we have been taught. How do we get unstuck from this debilitating self-talk? By exercising our creativity that is born from our humanity and allows us to build with our humanness. Our brains are meant to learn, grow, problem solve, and expand into its biggest, fullest, and brightest. *The present moment is our creation.* Let us create.

As children, we worked to turn dreams into reality. I used to ask my students all the time to dream big, and work hard to learn about themselves and the world around them. Why do we now as adults, just dream? It seems that as we get older, we find ourselves subscribing to the dominant culture's ideology that we are all just cogs in the giant machine of nationalism, hierarchy, and capitalism. Before we know it, we are so busy with bills and keeping up with the Amerikkkan Dream that we wake up one morning exhausted, and ready to retire. Now, this is a small percentage of folx. The majority have more downs than ups when it comes to just feeling good about oneself as a human being. All of this is enforced or upheld by the ideals of the status quo. Taking action to move away from this way of thinking is a great place to start.

When I look at my past, my education, and I see moments where I went beyond what I knew, I see the theater and dance program that I started at the school I also helped create. All of that was way beyond what I knew at that time, yet I took action.

I never really dreamed of myself being in a classroom. Once I got there though, LOOK OUT! I went much further than I thought I was capable of going: orchestrating student trips to Scotland with original shows for the Edinburgh Fringe Festival, working with other schools while in Scotland, establishing a dance program, inspiring an ever-increasing number of students to take my classes, and gratefully accepting the voluntary efforts of folx who supported us throughout this journey. And now, I have my own consulting business. The footprints I've left in all these places have opened my heart and world up to the creativity necessary to be on this journey.

I want everyone to explore their own personal adventure by creatively connecting with people. I want them to feel deeply that they have a purpose and feel confident enough to live their purpose. I want everyone to look out for each other and help one another find their own path. No two paths are the same, and I don't believe they were meant to be the same. I am moving humanity forward. I am moving humanity toward its ever-growing potential, taking into consideration oppressive forces along the way and finding ways to nullify and dull their effects on the individual. *The future is our inspiration.* Seven generations from now will be so much more than what humanity is currently, and I am excited for this. Moving from dreams into action.

As I stated before, there are many obstacles that have been thrown at me, and those obstacles bred apathy. I didn't dream, really, about any type of life. My suicide attempts were proof of that. When I grew beyond that time in life, and allowed myself to be educated by those moments, the dreaming began to happen.

I've shared with you in several ways how I have never felt true belonging. I wrote earlier that I never really dreamed of success in a certain area or of the perfect man or relationship. What I feel I've always wanted, which could be reinterpreted as dreamed, is to be somewhere, ANYWHERE, that I felt in my heart of hearts that I belonged.

I remember one of the first times, of many, that someone viciously told me to, "GO BACK TO WHERE YOU CAME FROM!" I was holding the hand of my older sister while walking to the store a few blocks away. We had just moved to the small town of Isanti, Minnesota. I was three or four years old. We were renting a house in town, while my father and mother figured out what it meant for this multi-ethnic family to be living in small-town rural Amerikkka.

There was a group of teenagers on bikes riding toward us, laughing. They mean-mugged us as they rode by. I heard them stop, so I tried turning around to look at them. My sister pulled my arm and said to keep looking forward. Soon I heard them coming up behind us pretty fast. My sister pulled me even further off the side of the road as they raced by yelling, "GO BACK TO WHERE YOU CAME FROM!" I didn't understand what they meant by those words, but I understood those words were said with anger and hatred. Lucky for them no racial slur was said, otherwise, I would have broken free from my sister, chased them down, and bopped them with my little fists, just like Mama had said to do when it came to the n-word. Situations like these, and there were a plethora of them, are why I have a deeply ingrained desire to find somewhere I belong.

Invitation: Gentle reminder to drink some water.

Humanity's growth has been stunted by the nightmare that is white-bodied supremacy. There is a culture that continues to perpetuate this white-bodied way of thinking. With the creation of race, racism, white, blackness, and the ideas that one race is superior to another, and all the atrocities that come with that way of thinking, the potential of humanity has been corrupted. Greed, monetary gain, senseless killing of one another in the name being seen as the most important … be it with some cloth, religion, or nation. It has all weakened what humanity could expand into.

Humanity's dreams were born out of darkness and what lurked in the dark. Many dream sequences that humans have recorded were mostly about nightmares. Situations filled with monsters, anxiety, fears, and heavily laden feelings of lack. It has driven humanity to want to be comfortable, which was later exacerbated by those that created ideas of power. We have land (that was stolen from its original peoples) and therefore we are powerful, comfortable. We have food, water, shelter, and the resources to create that for others (we will charge you handsomely for it) and therefore we are powerful, comfortable. Now we have hordes of people, generation after generation, dreaming to be in those constructed ideals of power, comfortable. Wake me up from THESE dreams!

Turning dreams of power into dreams of belonging will help humanity to expand into its biggest, fullest, and brightest.

My definition of biggest, fullest, and brightest: When a person believes in the truth of their human right to BE, allowing them to become their authentic self, the self that understands how the current status quo has manipulated the way they view themselves; the person is fully realized. Their human spirit takes on this idea of glowing, which becomes the brightest aspect of their authenticity.

I've begun, in these past few years, to dream of being fully realized as myself. That my inner light glows on the darkest of days. I am walking through the world being led by my humanity. It feels strong, confident, and powerful. By asking myself, "How much of your thinking is your thinking?" I am taking actionable steps daily to let this fully realized being transform from dream to reality. Embracing the transformation. I am my biggest, fullest, and brightest.

I've written throughout this book my lived experiences, many of which have been shared from my youth. These stories are woven together through my memories of how my cognitive brain decided to deal with and live this journey called life. How those times stretched me into being who I am today. It wasn't always something that felt good, while other times it was like a refreshing drink of cool water on a hot day.

I'm a firm believer that it is not necessary to always be going through trials and tribulations to understand your own, or someone else's, humanity. We didn't wake up one morning and go, "Oh, I am going to be a human after all."

When we move from the dream state of wanting all our basic needs met, to actually having our basic needs met, we free up so much energy to allow us to grow as a human being. Now, I'm not saying that one must amass wealth, material objects, and/or land. If we were all afforded the basic needs, I firmly believe that the shift in our consciousness as humans would be profound. And no, it can't be just spots of socialism here and there for this to be an epic shift. All humans must have all their basic needs met. This is when the biggest shift will occur. How do we get there? How do we go from dream to reality?

First step, personal transformation must occur.

Taking responsibility and holding ourselves and each other accountable for making sure everyone has the basics is as good a place as any to start. Will there be resistance? Of course, there will be. It wouldn't be authentic if it didn't have some resistance. Look at what the wealth gap, oppressive systems and the free market has done for humanity. They continue to loop financial gain and power into a small percentage of the population that uphold the ideas of the status quo. Causing humanity to be stuck in a catch-22. There is no dogma with this new action. Human beings have basic needs to survive and resources are in abundance on this planet. Everyone is deserving of life.

If we keep searching for medical advancements to extend our lives, technological advancements to "connect" over great distances, agricultural advancements in growing and reproduction of crops, and so forth, why wouldn't we just say, "Hey, everyone gets food, water, and shelter, no matter where you are in the world."

Makes sense to me, or am I just dreaming?

As we have journeyed through this book, and my lived experiences, it is clear to me that I am becoming more fully realized, not dreaming. I am willing to fully stand in my role as a BUILDER now, while being of service to all humanity, myself included, and for seven generations from now. I want to build a world where normal means nurturing our youth by actively listening to their stories. It looks like modeling for them accountability, integrity, respect, responsibility, and unconditional LOVE. It's reminding them, and ourselves, along the way to always strive to be our biggest, fullest, and brightest while helping others achieve the same. We are all worthy of this and have only begun to achieve our full potential as part of this beautiful, vast world.

Invitation: Now go live it. Think about how you can make some of your dreams a reality. Look back to the end of Chapter Eight at what you wrote down. Take a moment to plan what you are going to do. What steps are needed for that thing to get done? What can you accomplish today? Then put down the book and do that thing. Remember that this does not have to be a giant step, but even small steps can disrupt and dismantle the status quo.

ten

equity lens

~~I am crafting a world built upon the pillars of empathy, compassion, integrity, and unconditional love. I am being led by accountability, responsibility, and unconditional belonging. This empowers me to stand strong in all my authenticity, dignity, and strength that was passed down to me by my ancestors, so that I may model this for seven generations to come, so that we all may live our biggest, fullest, and brightest life.~~
~~(This is my current Equity Lens, and it is the thirteenth iteration. Yours should always be changing, shifting, transforming, and growing – right alongside you.)~~

I am crafting a world in which my humanity recognizes your humanity, and places our humanity in the forefront of our hearts and minds. The world I am crafting is guided by powerful skills such as integrity, vulnerability, responsibility, grace, and unconditional love. May we all recognize that the past is our education, the future is our inspiration, and that the present moment is our creation so that we may support seven generations to come to BE their biggest, fullest, and brightest.

(This is my current Equity Lens, and it is the nineteenth iteration. I changed it right before this book went to print. I left the old one here so you can see that Yours should always be changing, shifting, transforming, and growing – right alongside you.)

As I continue to not only read my Equity Lens several times each day, but also actually put it into action, I have noticed that foundational pillars keep coming to the surface. These pillars are based on my personal virtues and values that my lived experiences have shown to be integral in the truth of my authenticity. It has taken many hours of personal Work in the shape of the dances I've choreographed, my spoken word and one-man show performances, and hours of therapy to develop a deeper understanding and belief that I am worthy of living my authenticity. To be able to uphold my authentic self, I rely on my foundational pillars. Let's look at them. Remember, these are my pillars, forged from my lived experiences. My Truth Vision. Some of my pillars may inspire your pillars, and some may feel relatively distant from your lived experiences. That is beautiful.

A strong foundational Equity Lens pillar, and one that is used for moving from dreamlandia into actual action, is **belonging**. Not just the kind that is being built, but it also needs to include a personal feeling of belonging. Through the chapters, I've shared my personal growth by shining a light on the lived experiences that fed my Shadows. Over the years, I began to not only desire/dream of belonging, but I began to craft it for those around me, and, finally, for myself as well. Do you feel deserving of belonging? Do you feel you deserve belonging everywhere you go? If neuroscience has shown us that the brain desires a sense of belonging, shouldn't belonging be a basic human necessity? Again, what kind of world could we build if we all felt lovingly, unconditionally supported with a strong sense of belonging? This is a deeply rooted pillar of my Equity Lens.

We discussed in-depth in Chapter Three how important it is for one to **be within integrity to one's authentic self.** Once we have allowed ourselves to build belonging, it is important that we reside within this unconditional belonging from a place of authenticity. No need to hide, push away, mask, ignore, or numb any aspect of yourself. It will all have a place within a structure that has unconditional belonging as one of its pillars. Now, you have read parts of my journey and you know that it hasn't been easy by any stretch of the imagination. With the path that humanity has been on, we all have personal Work to do. Doing the Work allows us to believe we deserve the truth of who we are and then to build structures, systems, policies, and procedures that afford future generations the same truth of self. Being within integrity to your authenticity is a deeply rooted Equity Lens pillar for me.

Another one of my Equity Lens pillars is **unconditional love**.

Unconditional love is wrapped up in Christian religious vitriol and needs to be freed from those confines. Most people feel that the concept of unconditional love can only come through Jesus. I will define it in my own language so that folx can have another perspective from which to view these words together.

For myself, it is as simple as: You are human, and I will love you unconditionally from that perspective. Now, if you are causing other humans unnecessary duress or stress, oppressing others to amass personal wealth, and/or simply dehumanizing another for personal gain, I will shine a light on that injustice. It doesn't mean I don't have love for you as another human. It means that I will show you that all human beings are worthy of love and belonging, even if you're an asshole. Like my mama always said, "You have to love everyone, but you don't have to like them." I have made this my own by adding on to it: I love ya, but that doesn't mean I will be inviting you over for dinner.

All the pillars are interconnected. Their intersectional aspects are clear to me as I continue to recognize and honor them. This intersectionality created the pillar of **authenticity**. All signs around me point to growing in my authenticity: support of close loving friends and community, finances to get me started, mental support with my therapist, physical support training with a dear friend of over twenty years, and spirit support from acknowledging how grateful and humble I am for everything I just wrote. I am doing things differently just by humbly honoring how different I am on this part of my journey than I've ever been before. I have a stronger sense of self-worth, skill sets, and power of leading from my heart/purpose. I am leading from my own Equity Lens. It isn't just read or recited. I am fully living it, and because of that choice, I am viewing and building a world never envisioned or built before. I am serving humanity. I am serving seven generations from now. I am of service. I am leading with my purpose and that is carving out space for me to elevate. Asking people to help by using their skill set, while helping them find their purpose, is a different approach than my past. This will help me continue creating the results I'm seeing and want in my life. I am feeling my power rise as my clarity brings into focus my purpose. My elevation has begun.

Once the pillars have been crafted, it is important to understand that **loving yourself is at the deepest core of turning dreams into action**. The gaslighting and divide and conquer tools of white cisgendered supremacy culture have made it so most people don't even recognize their own humanity, let alone someone else's. Doubting my own self-worth has allowed others to not only question my worthiness, but my humanity as well. How can I take actionable steps on the dreams of liberation, justice, and equity if I don't believe I deserve those very things?

It's like when folx say, "I am good at telling everyone else what to do, but I can't take my own advice!"

Here's that moment. Take your own advice and love yourself the way you keep telling other people to do. Once we start doing that, we will realize that our dreams are worthy of action. That we all deserve to have our basic needs met without duress. Humanity deserves to be fully realized for what it can BE, and not just what it dreams.

My definition of an Equity Lens: Something crafted by the individual, utilizing their own lived experiences. It must be ever-evolving as one meets new people, has new experiences, gains knowledge and wisdom, and recognizes what their own definition of anti-racist work is. It must be something that grows into being Your Truth Vision. It has integrity, accountability, responsibility, vulnerability, hard work, self-worth, and unconditional love at its core. It's building unconditional belonging. It is a CALL TO ACTION! With my current Equity Lens, I'm able to see through the dominant cultures ideas to help me heal from an oppressive society. This healing is guiding me towards how to build a more just and equity-filled world. A world where soft skills are seen as power skills, and emotional intelligence helps us to be more humanity-led. The use of my Equity Lens helps bring me back to the center of my spiral, grounded, more often than not.

Should everyone craft their own personal Equity Lens? Yes. At its very core, it allows a person to truly begin liberating themselves from the oppressive confines of the status quo. It gives folx a tool to use daily to help dig out, hammer together, smooth, and round the edges of what the world has told them they should be, and allow their authentic self to … BE.

As you have traveled through the pages of this book, being asked to reflect, move, breathe, and stretch into your authenticity, my personal Equity Lens has been there the entire time. It's been guiding me, encouraging me to go deeper, urging me to question my own truth, asking, "How much of your thinking is your thinking?" And I am grateful for it all, and the connections internally and externally.

Connection is another foundational pillar of my Equity Lens. Neuroscience has shown that our desire for a place to belong happens through connection to others, places, objects, traditions, and rituals. As I utilize my Equity Lens to build unconditional belonging, I have connected more with my authentic self, the world around me, and the world I am crafting, along with connecting to so many new people.

Please take a moment and reflect. What do you feel connected to/with? Are you feeling a stronger connection to your authentic self?

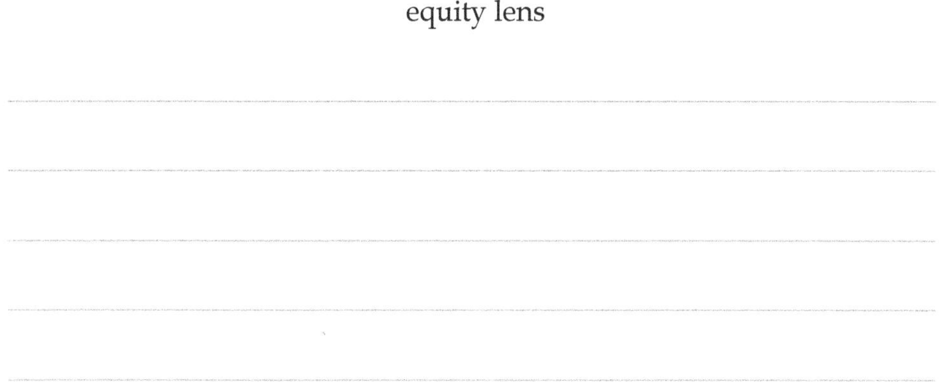

More and more people are feeling the shift happening in the world today: climate change, proximity through technology, divide and conquer, coveting wealth when there is plenty for all. It seems that for so long I've been in survival mode, trying my best to not believe the status quo and its ideas of me, and doing my best to not be indoctrinated into what it deems as successful. I, and many others, are coming out the other side of that way of thinking. I'm seeing that what we, as a society, started to call "normal" is more a death sentence.

- Death of our own perceptions through indoctrination.
- Death of joy and happiness due to the amount of time spent working.
- Death of our planet.
- Death of our lived experiences.

Enough with death, it is time to live. Through the creation of my Equity Lens, I am living life. Through the creation of my Equity Lens, I am dismantling white supremacy culture.

As I put my Equity Lens on and my *Truth Vision* is activated, it is easy for me to see *The Matrix* that makes up supremacy culture. I look at the world around me and see how dehumanizing our status quo is and how our indoctrination system feeds into this notion.

My vision is becoming clearer, and by using my Equity Lens I can dismantle and build at the same time, while making sure that I am not rebuilding that which has already been built. And most of all, I want to be rebuilding systems and structures that support the expansion of humanity; while being caring, loving, and sustainable for Earth.

There are many people, culturally and individually, who see humanity's connection to Earth. It is important for us to understand through our quest for liberation, justice, and equity that we also include the very thing that gives us life, while keeping us alive. Our planet is an integral part of finding a humanity-led society.

Patience is another foundational pillar. I've become more intimately aware of my lack of and/or abundance of patience, and have begun a deeper practice with it since crafting my Equity Lens. The ideas of speed, hurry up, productivity over quality, are all based in the white supremacy insecurity culture. Being in a hurry works against the expansion of the whole of humanity. A false sense of urgency seems to have greed at its core, thus allowing life to be controlled by fear. Fear of not getting it done on time, not getting enough done, not living up to the status quo's quotient of what's acceptable in the greater scheme of what an Amerikkkan must achieve. Fear is easy money! –filled with users and con artists. I used to con myself into believing many of these ideologies, thinking that if I just worked myself to death, then they would see my worth and maybe, just maybe, I would see my worth as well.

I have since then learned to trust my instincts again, which is no easy task since supremacy culture doesn't want you to. Through patience, I've learned to trust my Equity Lens and its ever-evolving aspects. It has given me the patience to truly grow into my *Truth Vision*. It's interesting to see how patience has deepened my call to action. Out of patience has come my personal Work. Patience for my own transformation, and patience for believing that people, Equity Lens or not, are coming from their own lived experiences and starting points. I'm not sabotaging myself anymore or panicking when time keeps on ticking.

With this patience, a kind of harmony is filling my life. Harmony with my authentic self, with the world around me, and with the world I am crafting. This evolution has been on a spiritual level as well.

My Equity Lens has been helping me develop my intuitive side; my spiritual level. My instincts have suffered the most by being gaslit throughout my life. Being told that I was making things up, being lied to, or yelled at, told that I must not love them because my instincts are raising red flags, has caused me to question everything I say and do. My instincts weren't allowed to be true to my authentic self. Reading, crafting, and developing my Equity Lens has me trusting my truth more and more each and every day. I believe that our intuitive side is a deeper connection to Earth and the world around us. It is the side that we sometimes feel we must hurry away from, to not be seen as some of the dehumanizing things we ourselves have said about other humans.

Belonging, *Integrity*, *Unconditional Love*, *Authenticity*, *Loving Yourself*, *Connection*, and *Patience*—these pillars have become the foundation of my lived experiences moving forward. Not only are they strong on their own, but now that I have seen, felt, and heard their interconnectedness, I've been able to fully stand in my authenticity. My Equity Lens is a tool that I constantly use.

My Equity Lens has helped me remember my power. The dominant culture has convinced us that amassing wealth, land, material objects, intelligence, even faith and religion, gives us power, and/or renders us powerless. With my Equity Lens, I am able to stay connected to the power that every human being, and every creature and plant on this planet, was born with. Remember in Chapter Two when I spoke about the "light" we all are born with? If we seek illumination, it will always be there for us.

I consider my Equity Lens to be "knowledgeable action." It is this knowledge that guides me toward crafting a world led by humanity. It is motivation to balance mind, body, and spirit. It is the will, on certain days, to just get out of bed, and on other days, the self-awareness to know that staying under the covers is just as fine.

One of the things that influences those "under the covers" kind of days is the indoctrination that we've all gone through. As we grew up and were pushed through the educational system, we were conditioned into the dominant culture's ideas of our nation, of each other, and how we move through these constructs. It's important when building toward a vision of justice that we understand how we might still be upholding these ideals of the dominant culture. We need to self-reflect on our own thinking and make sure we aren't just rebuilding the same thing.

Invitation: Set a timer for two minutes. Then stand in the starfish pose, with your legs wider than your shoulders and your hands above your head and spread out. Take this moment to take up space, to expand.

I'm choosing to expand into my Equity Lens. I've come to some of these conclusions about my Equity Lens because I've taken a deep dive into unpacking the concepts of internalized capitalism, internalized superiority, internalized racism, and internalized racial oppressions. These concepts afforded me deeper insights around generational trauma of my own, and others. They showed me that implicit bias is just the tip of the iceberg, and there's a lot more under that water. These "internalized" concepts show how intimate the Work for each individual truly is. This intimate Work can't be dealt with in the exact same way as another. It was important for me to continually ask myself, 'How much of my thinking is my thinking?' along with, 'What here is mine to own?' And if it isn't mine to own, how do I rid myself of this intrusive, false way of thinking? I do it by reading my Equity Lens every day, and multiple times a day. Your Equity Lens truly demands your *Truth Vision* upfront.

If we are not being truthful with ourselves, it will become clear as to how we aren't when using our Equity Lens. Using your Equity Lens brings integrity to yourself and into your daily life.

Balancing mind, body, and spirit. Past, present, future. Seven generations from now.

No greater action can be undertaken than to shift the consciousness of humanity. I will not try to cover up that fact. Your Equity Lens helps humanity look at the path it is currently on; a path steered by the dominant culture. The dominant culture has not allowed, nor will it ever allow, humanity to expand. The advancement of technology and science is pigeonholed by the dominant culture. The wealth it generates is more important than how it helps humanity to expand. It does this by keeping the wealthy wealthy, and the poor poor, with the thoughts that humanity must stay this course. Your Equity Lens is a direct disruption of said course.

I've been asked what makes me think folx are ready to let go of their concepts of right and wrong, good and evil, black and white, and go through the difficult task of building something NEW. I believe that once humanity truly recognizes its own personal empowerment through the shift in consciousness, people will bring upon themselves the necessary transformation that allows humanity to expand into its biggest, fullest, and brightest.

Weeding out past beliefs or ideas that upheld our own demise is another benefit of an Equity Lens. It isn't about living in judgment of self or others. It is being brave enough to be self-reflective, ask difficult questions, have a growth mindset, and begin to build the NEW. I continually capitalize NEW because it needs to come from a place we have yet to BE. I do not want the future to only come from one group or person's idea. It's going to take all of us recognizing each other's humanity, desire for belonging, and personal understanding of our own humanness.

As people continue to heed the call to action and begin building belonging, justice will lead us into the new normal. A world that has our own ideas of belonging in it, helping each other to grow, experience joy, and celebrate each other's humanity, and allows each person to know for themselves what living their biggest, fullest, and brightest means. I no longer want to be reactive to being dehumanized by the culture of white insecurity. I no longer want to constantly be on the defensive. I want to build the NEW. I want to leave tools and structures that help future generations to continue valuing their courageous creativity. Being led by their very own humanity. No more survival mode for anyone. GET OUT OF THE COMFORT ZONE. IT'S A TRAP!

When am I courting my fears by fighting Shadow and all of

its negative ideas? Fighting is the key word here.

I've learned from my Equity Lens that there are times when pushing up my sleeves to throw hands with my negative thoughts is just the workout I need. I've also learned that sometimes I need to come at these negative ideas with a strong sense of gentleness. That's right, gentleness.

Gentleness is not weakness. It's another facet of being human. Remember, we've all been indoctrinated into the status quo, and on some level still operate from its constructs on a daily basis. To balance the fight, switch it up and come at it with gentleness.

You see, when I am fighting, it might only be because I am projecting my fears onto others. I might just be fearing the other person because they are exactly what I am fearing about myself. At the base of all this might simply be the fact that I am not loving myself the way I deserve and therefore cannot let go of my fears. Self-actualization, self-awareness, and self-love all reside inside my Equity Lens. To balance my power, I must show myself the same love and compassion I want for all humanity. I am worthy.

breathe
It all seems so blurry to me
breathe
Clarity is what I need

breathe
Something's coming into focus
breathe
What is this hocus pocus?

breathe
It is all so very new
breathe
Can we really make this true?

breathe
Just a little bit deeper

breathe
Is this hill getting steeper?

breathe
I see it all so clearly now
breathe
Work, dedication, that's how

breathe
And let it all transform

biggest, fullest, brightest

Hovering above the earth
Doing this with my mind
Seeing others up here
We have all done our time

Time we spent listening to the void
The void of status quo, No! You will not grow
Grow into what you are meant to be
You will grow into what we see
We see you as a cog in the machine
Something that takes away all that is green
Representation or literally
Of what is needed for me to be me

Throughout the Work I've done, I've found many things to help me find my inner strength and that are necessary for me to be me. I hope that you have experienced, encountered, and adopted tools to help you create what is needed for you to be you, and also that this reflection has gotten a bit easier for you. None of the things I've written about have happened for me overnight. Most of this is a result of Work, as well as meeting with therapists, friends, lovers, and colleagues. It is a result of looking inside, never settling for the easy way out, and instead striving to find what I need to feel my biggest, fullest, and brightest. Through this wonderful journey of exploration (of life), I've discovered five things I need in order to show up with inner strength:

- Living my truth, my purpose
- Facing/loving/learning from my Shadow
- Allowing my heart to love and be loved
- Being creative, writing
- Leading with love

I tossed around the idea of explaining each of these in greater detail. But I realized I have done this already throughout the pages of this book. I also want you to see these five things for what they mean to your lived experiences. I never want to just tell people how to live their life, but to extend an invitation for them to explore their truth. May you continue to feel curiosity to be creative about this life you are here to live.

Take a moment to reflect on what is needed for you to be YOU.

I need to give myself permission to be my biggest, fullest, and brightest. This means stepping fully into being a guide, storyteller, influencer, builder, and healer. I balance mind, body, and spirit. I engage with people who feel drawn to crafting their personal Equity Lens. I currently live in Hawai'i. This move has allowed me to have laughter, joy, and peace surrounding me. There is so much green-growth! — all around me. I hear the rain on the roof, see ancient ferns grow to massive heights, and smell the delicious aromas of food being cooked as they fill my home. All of this is nourishing the mind, body, and spirit. I have impacted thousands of lives in my time as a performer and educator—audiences and students. I am now impacting people who are crafting their Equity Lens. Activating my biggest dreams. … BIGGEST, FULLEST, BRIGHTEST!

I believe that we, as humans, can be so much more. More in the sense of inner potential coming forward and into the world. The magic that we cultivated when we were more connected to this planet and all its wonders is not gone. In previous chapters, I've written about the ways we have been forced, and/or have willingly gone down a path that doesn't support us evolving into our biggest, fullest, and brightest. Through sharing my lived experiences, I have shown you what I mean about being in different places on the spiral, by sharing *shifts* with you, in various forms. Becoming your biggest, fullest, and brightest is not a goal post. It is not a "get there and you win an award." Instead, it is the center of your own spiral that you will continue to travel to throughout the course of your life.

Your biggest, fullest, and brightest is the place where you can be unapologetically, authentically, and truthfully YOU. I am not here to tell you that this is easy, that once you find that center you can stay there forever. That is not true for me or for anyone I know. So often you will find yourself spiraled from the center whether that is due to Shadow, white cisgendered supremacy culture or you just didn't get enough sleep last night. But I will tell you that the more you can find your biggest, fullest, and brightest (your center), the easier it is to lovingly come back to it. Effortless Authenticity.

Biggest. I remember being told by one of my first color guard instructors that we needed to be as big as possible when out on the field. We had to express ourselves to the very top of the bleachers and beyond. How was a judge sitting at the top of the stadium supposed to feel anything if we weren't our biggest selves? I have never forgotten that. I passed it along to color guards that I was fortunate enough to work with. I passed it along in different iterations to my theater students, dance students, and now to humanity.

Fullest. When I use the term *fullest* it is directly linked to being a lifelong learner. Learning about ourselves, the world around us, the people in our lives and those who we may never come into contact with will help each of us to fill our cup to overflowing. Always learning, always growing. I believe our stomachs can become uncomfortably full, yet I don't believe that humanity has even begun to see how "full" we can get on living an authentic and truthful life.

Brightest. Yes, my friends, shine brightly! There are many things in this world that have a dulling effect on physical spaces, situations we find ourselves in, and our personal overall outlook on self and the world around us. With a balance of mind, body, and spirit, a person just seemingly glows, giving off this energy of brilliance. It isn't easily put into words, yet it can easily be lived. Once again, looking at my Equity Lens, digging deeper into personal reflection, my Work toward authenticity, and overall acceptance of my worth and dignity, will always bring about my brightest shine.

I believe there've been moments of each, such as during my students' performances, listening intently to someone whose words ignite my cells, and being in a natural setting with the energies of the flora and fauna feeding me sustenance. I believe that if I didn't have to fight for my survival at times, I'd be in a more constant state of biggest, fullest, and brightest.

Living my biggest, fullest, and brightest reminds me to

reclaim and stand strong in my personal power, and for that I am grateful. The dominant culture tries to tell us what power is, who will always have that power, and who gets to wield it. Nah. We're all born with power. Our bodies generate electrical impulses. See? Power!

Remember, sometimes it isn't that simple. Having to wade through the mire the dominant culture has created, figuratively and literally, is part of its plan to divide and conquer. Except it's dividing us from the truth of who we are rather than merely dividing us apart from one another.

Listen closely for those moments throughout your day when you, yourself, don't recognize your own humanity: toxic self-talk, no boundaries, giving your soul power. Listen deeply for the pathway back to the lost treasure — your personal power.

May we all practice soul care and mindfulness, moments of stillness, so that we may listen deeply for where we hide our treasures.

"My strength is my authenticity." When I turned thirty, I was living in Amsterdam. My father had recently been diagnosed with COPD and emphysema. He asked if I would come home for my birthday. I did.

My father felt the need to show his love through material things. A run-down snowmobile, boat, camper, dirt bike, and his biggest purchase—some acreage on a lake in north central Minnesota. We called it "up North."

I figured I would invite close friends up North for my thirtieth birthday. It was a wonderful time. Giggling, laughing, partying, and really just enjoying each other's company. It was lovingly joyous.

On the last day, only my father and I remained up North. We decided to take the boat out fishing one more time. In his later years, the fishing trips became the one thing he remembered about raising us kids. It was the "good" he did while raising a family.

"One more cast and we should probably head back in. Sun's going down."

I am eyeing a tree that had fallen into the lake when my father says, "You should cast over by those cattails."

I decide to cast between the two. Just like that, I couldn't have scripted it for a movie any better, 7.5 lbs. largemouth bass jumps taking my lure into his big old mouth. My heart rate is up, smiling so big it hurts, and I look over at my father, and he has the same big grin. Five minutes later we land the bass and head back into the cabin.

"You caught it. You clean it." My father says with a small smirk. But first he has to take the obligatory photo, the one that cuts off the heads of everyone in the picture, but the bass looked good!

It's after dinner. I'm doing the dishes while my father is laying down on the bed in the back bedroom. Just as I'm finishing, I hear him coming to the front of the cabin. The energy has changed from the jovial energy of earlier. It is much more subdued. I'm thinking that it is because we both are full of fish, and, for a man that is ill, he expended a lot of energy that day.

"Son. I think I am the reason that you and your brother are gay."

Every cell in my body reacts as if I had been struck by lightning. Chaos churns just under my skin with the deep recognition of what it is he is saying. He is trying to tell me that he is gay. My father wants to discuss his sexuality with me. Everything is loud in my head, and I'm feeling anxious all of a sudden. *Must get out … must get out … must …*

"Dad, don't worry about my brother and me. We don't blame you. I am going to go outside and have a smoke."

I rush outside into the darkness. I light a cigarette. I think of the feelings I just had. "He didn't say that he was. What makes you think? Why can't you talk with him? It probably isn't that. You're just …" Ten cigarettes later my father sticks his head out of the door and says he is going to bed.

"Goodnight, Dad."

"Goodnight, Son."

Jump ahead four years. It's my birthday again. I am turning thirty-four. I've rushed home two days earlier because my father has been admitted into the hospital, and I am told it probably won't be long now. My mother gets a call from the hospital. Seems my father won't let the female nurses bathe and shave him, and the one male nurse who has been doing it has the day off. My mom turns to my brother and me, "Will you go up to the hospital and bathe and shave your father, please?" We say yes, and we are off. I have two brothers. It happens to be my gay brother with me.

We get to the hospital, and I'm instantly struck with the smells, sounds, and sterile whiteness of the hallways and rooms. I am triggered. Memories of my youth, like being rushed there for stitches on several occasions.

"Hey, Dad! We heard you wanted a bath and a shave?"

"What?!? Yes, yes, I surely do."

"Don't worry, Dad, we got you."

My brother and I clean our father, and shave his stubbly face. My brother leaves the room for some reason, I can't remember why. That same feeling washes over me …

"Son. I think I am the reason that you and your brother are gay."

This time my instincts are screaming, full force, into every cell of my being that "he wants to tell you his story." His story about him being gay.

More calm this time, as I pick up his hand and hold it in mine, "Dad, don't worry about my brother and me. We don't blame you. I have always known, ever since I was little and you sent me to camp."

I can see it there in his eyes. The voice inside me is saying, "I am so sorry, Dad. I just can't have that conversation with you. I am not sure when I will ever be able to." I changed the subject.

"I have a performance back in Seattle tomorrow. My flight leaves later this evening. I am headed to the airport. You going to be alright?"

"Yup. I sure am. I love you."

"I love you too, Dad."

On my flight home, the day after my birthday, I felt him leave this world. August 5, 2003. I turned around and headed back to Minnesota. There was this part of me that was so relieved he wasn't suffering anymore. Then there was the part of me that needed reminding that I didn't possess the tools to have that conversation with him. Who was I to have THAT conversation with my dad?!?

Invitation: Please take a moment and take a sip of water.

It's 2021. I am writing my first book, and I've created a company based on what my soul has to share with the rest of humanity. That company's offering to humanity is to help folx create, build, and wield a tool. A tool that is shifting the consciousness of humanity. The offering: Crafting Your Equity Lens. The tool: Your Personal Equity Lens. In my life so far, my journey has given me many tools. To all the therapists, friends, lovers, colleagues in the Work, fellow educators, family — chosen and blood, I'm so very grateful to you all for allowing me to explore my truth. Through my lived experiences, I am creating and using my Equity Lens to become my authentic self.

Dad, I want you to know that my authentic self is ready to listen. When you passed from this existence, I had come to terms with the abuse I had experienced from you. I realized that you didn't have any tools in your toolkit to deal with the truth of your lived experiences. What you knew was that to love us children, you had to give. You gave away the truth of who you were. I forgive you.

Now, as I struggle on certain days, am grateful on other days, and full of love at the end of it all, I want to sit with you and listen. I want to hear your truth. I want you to see that you were worthy of that truth. That your dignity was never in question. That your authentic self would have thrived in this world that I am creating. I only wanted to see you live your biggest, fullest, and brightest life.

With all my heart,
Matthew

I am ARRIVING, right when I am supposed to be.
This arrival is allowing me to BE.
BE brave.
BE authentic.
BE in service.
BE ALIVE.
BE LOVE.
BE strong.
BE confident.
BE POWERFUL.
BElieve in YOUrself.
BE YOU

1. Loving v. Virginia, 388 U.S. 1 (1967).

2. Brené Brown, Braving the Wilderness: The Quest for True Belonging and the Courage to Stand Alone (New York: Random House, 2017), 40 and 157. Kindle. Used by permission of The Random House Group Limited and Random House, an imprint and division of Penguin Random House LLC. All rights reserved.

3. J. L. King and Karen Hunter, On the Down Low: A Journey into the Lives of 'Straight' Black Men Who Sleep with Men (New York: Harlem Moon, 2005).

4. Jamie Sams and David Carson, Medicine Cards: The Discovery of Power Through the Ways of Animals, rev. ed. (New York: St. Martin's/Farrar, Straus and Giroux, 1999).

5. Oxford Advanced American Dictionary, online. "Integrity," https://www.oxfordlearnersdictionaries.com/us/definition/american_english/integrity#:~:text=integrity-,noun,a%20man%20of%20great%20integrity

6. Jason Reynolds and Ibram X. Kendi, Stamped: Racism, Antiracism, and You (Waterville, ME: Thorndike, 2020), 3. Reprinted by permission of Little, Brown Books for Young Readers, an imprint of Hachette Book Group, Inc.

7. James Baldwin, Nobody Knows My Name: More Notes of a Native Son (Beacon Press, 1955/1983). Reprinted with permission from Beacon Press, Boston, Massachusetts.

8. Teju Ravilochan, Vidya Ravilochan, and Colette Kessler, "Could the Blackfoot Wisdom that Inspired Maslow Guide Us Now?" GatherFor, April 2021, https://gatherfor.medium.com/maslow-got-it-wrong-ae45d6217a8c&sa=D&source=docs&ust=1643072241112364&

usg=AOvVaw1fOLWcjyrBz3wOSxB9v_dk.

9. Parker Palmer, The Courage to Teach: Exploring the Inner Landscape of a Teacher's Life, 2nd ed. (San Francisco: Jossey-Bass, 2007), 104. Kindle. Reprinted with permission of John Wiley & Sons, Inc.

10. Palmer, The Courage to Teach.

11. Eliott C. McLaughlin, "An officer pleads guilty in a choking incident, and an ex-NFL prospect struggles to put his life back together," CNN, October 7, 2020, https://edition.cnn.com/2020/10/06/us/desmond-marrow-choking-police-aftermath/index.html.

12. Seth Wickersham, "The view from within," ESPN, August 26, 2011, https://www.espn.com/nfl/story/_/id/6898043/nfl-michael-vick-548-days-bars-espn-magazine.

13. Bill Chappell, "Brock Turner Freed From Jail After Serving Half Of 6-Month Sentence," npr, September 2, 2016, https://www.npr.org/sections/thetwo-way/2016/09/02/492390163/brock-turner-freed-from-jail-after-serving-half-of-6-month-sentence.

14. Sams and Carson, Medicine Cards, 2-4.

15. Resmaa Menakem, "Notice the Rage; Notice the Silence," On Being with Krista Tippett, June 4, 2020, https://onbeing.org/programs/resmaa-menakem-notice-the-rage-notice-the-silence/. Reprinted with permission.

16. Loving v. Virginia, 388 U.S. 1 (1967).

17. Brené Brown, The Gifts of Imperfection (Center City, MN: Hazelden, 2010), 25. Used with permission of Hazelden Foundation, from The gifts of imperfection: let go of who you think you're supposed to be and embrace who you are, Brené C. Brown, 2010; permission conveyed through Copyright Clearance Center, Inc.

18. [Matthew Reynolds], "Crafting Your Equity Lens," Matthew Reynolds Consulting, www.mrrconsulting.org. A tool that, when used, grows into being a person's Truth Vision.

19. M. Scott Peck, M.D., P.C. The Different Drum: Community Making and Peace (New York: Touchstone, 1987), 59. Reprinted with the permission of Touchstone, a division of Simon & Schuster, Inc. All rights reserved.

20. Peck, The Different Drum, 61-76.

gratitude

Matthew Reynolds: The list of GRATITUDE would be another book. I have been fortunate to meet some genuine, authentic, loving, magical beings throughout my life's journey thus far: Trena Bolden Fields who sparked the writing of this book, those who read pages and gave feedback, people whose generosity, Krystal Meisel and Mary Moody founders of Hawai'i Lit, helped the completion of the book, you all are in my heart, and have moved my soul. Thank you for being in my life. And now, YOU, the reader have become yet another one.

Brittnee, this wouldn't have been possible if you weren't open to listening to my sometimes crazy, oftentimes heart driven ideas about education and how I was navigating this world. Your guidance in wordsmithing this book has been magical and invaluable. I am so looking forward to our next book adventure(s). Thank you for being in my life.

Brittnee Zwirn: I would like to take a moment to thank Matthew Reynolds for this opportunity. For being a great friend, listener, colleague, coach, mentor, and the list can go on. He has encouraged me from day one of my teaching career to be unapologetically idealistic and to never settle just because the system tells you to. I am looking forward to our future collaborations!

I want to also thank my husband, Angelo, for being my biggest supporter, best friend and the person that gently reminds me to turn off my work brain and to have some fun! I love you!

Lastly, Dear Reader, thank you for picking up this book. Thank you for taking the time to do the Work. It will never be easy, but this is what HUMANITY deserves, this is what YOU deserve. I am in awe of your willingness to fight against the status quo and to demand better for yourself, for others and for our future generations. Thank you.

the authors

Matthew Reynolds is an equity consultant, educator and warrior for justice. With over fifteen years of experience as a teacher in secondary education and a passion for the arts and disseminating information, Matthew has tuned his ability to reach minds and hearts through learning and processing. Matthew regularly shares his message of liberated diversity, equity and inclusion in talks with organizations and on social media. He has been interviewed on The Jefferson Exchange - Jefferson Public Radio, The People Impact Podcast and The Keenest Observers- Jefferson Public Radio on Culturally Responsive Teaching. He believes that everyone is deserving of love and belonging. Matthew helps people craft their Equity Lens. This tool is a call to action and guides people towards living their biggest, fullest, and brightest. You can learn more at www.mrrconsulting.org.

Brittnee Zwirn graduated from Southern Oregon University with a bachelors' in criminology and criminal justice as well as a Master of Arts in teaching. She lives and teaches high school in Southern Oregon. When not writing with Matthew, Brittnee enjoys baking bread, kayaking and spending time with her husband, Angelo; son, Leo; and her pets, Harvey and Zoey.

About Bolden Fields Publishing

We provide publishing services for educators and consultants who want to publish a book that will make a positive impact on our communities. Our hope is that our works will positively impact humanity for the better. We provide print and digital works and publishing services to help transform lives.

For more information about Bolden Fields Publishing, please visit www.boldenfieldspublishing.com.